The Business Coach

Action International
Business Coaching

Other Books in the Instant Success Series

Successful Franchising by Bradley J. Sugars
The Real Estate Coach by Bradley J. Sugars
Billionaire in Training by Bradley J. Sugars
Instant Cashflow by Bradley J. Sugars
Instant Sales by Bradley J. Sugars
Instant Leads by Bradley J. Sugars
Instant Profit by Bradley J. Sugars
Instant Promotions by Bradley J. Sugars
Instant Repeat Business by Bradley J. Sugars
Instant Team Building by Bradley J. Sugars
Instant Systems by Bradley J. Sugars
Instant Referrals by Bradley J. Sugars
Instant Advertising by Bradley J. Sugars

The
Business
Coach

BRADLEY J. SUGARS

McGraw-Hill

New York   Chicago   San Francisco   Lisbon   London
Madrid   Mexico City   Milan   New Delhi   San Juan
Seoul   Singapore   Sydney   Toronto

4 5 6 7 8 9 0 DOC/DOC 0 9 8 7

ISBN 0-07-146672-X

This publication is designed to provide accurate and authoritative information in regard to the subject matter covered. It is sold with the understanding that neither the author nor the publisher is engaged in rendering legal, accounting, or other professional service. If legal advice or other expert assistance is required, the services of a competent professional person should be sought.
—From a Declaration of Principles jointly adopted by Committee of the American Bar Association and a Committee of Publishers.

McGraw-Hill books are available at special quantity discounts to use as premiums and sales promotions, or for use in corporate training programs. For more information, please write to the Director of Special Sales, McGraw-Hill Professional, Two Penn Plaza, New York, NY 10121-2298. Or contact your local bookstore.

Library of Congress Cataloging-in-Publication Data

Sugars, Bradley J.
    The business coach / Bradley J. Sugars.—1st ed.
        p.   cm.
    ISBN 0-07-146672-X (alk. paper)
    1. Executive coaching.   2. Mentoring in business.   I. Title.
    HD30.4.S78 2006
    658.4'07124—dc22   2005025280

Dedicated to my Coaches—You know who you are.

■ CONTENTS

∎ INTRODUCTION

Growing your own business can be an incredibly rewarding, amazing experience.

It can be.

But for most, it's not.

That's why when I started the Business Coaching industry back in 1993, I was overwhelmed with people wanting, no needing, my help.

Today, with literally hundreds of Business Coaches on the *Action International* team in 18 countries, we have developed such a powerful system for growing both companies and the people in them that we want to share it with you.

Whether your challenge is that you have no time left for a life outside of business, no ability to get good people or, just simply, that you need to boost or even create bottom-line profits, through this book you will see the system we at *Action International* Business Coaching walk people through day in and day out to create great companies.

Problems in business are all a symptom of a company that has grown without control. Without a plan or a step-by-step process that companies should follow when they're growing. Companies who have not met the Business Coach.

I am a business owner and I have taught thousands of business owners how to do this, and my aim is to make it as simple for you as I can. There's still hard work involved, but at least you'll know what you should be doing.

As you follow Joe and Nellie through the path of growing their small business, remember that it doesn't matter what style or type of business you are in. What matters is that you grasp the core principles, the underlying strategies that can help grow any business, in any marketplace.

My coaching team has coached almost every type of business in every type of marketplace, from central China to central Colorado. The strategies are the same; it's just the people that change.

I truly hope that you not only read this book and follow it, but that you recommend it to or buy it for your friends in business. They really will thank you for it.

Brad Sugars

P.S. If you would like to meet with one of my coaching team to see if we can help grow your business, you'll see a special offer in the back of this book.

The Business Coach
Mind Map

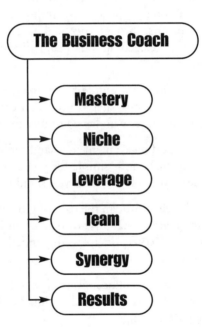

The Business Coach

Mastery

Niche

Leverage

Team

Synergy

Results

The door swung open and in he strode.

"Hi, Nellie, how are you doing?" the man asked, as he made his way past shelves packed with freshly baked bread to the counter.

"Good to see you, Pete. And how are things with you?"

"Fantastic. Never been better. And you want to know the best part? It gets better each day."

Nellie was stunned by his obvious zest for life. And as she had done ever since school days when she first met Pete and his best friend Joe, she found herself warming to him. Funny how he still had that "something," she thought. For her it had always been a toss up between Pete and Joe, yet she never really regretted marrying Joe. She often wondered whether Pete knew any of this.

"Same as usual, Pete?" she asked, turning to the shelf behind her.

"Yes, same as always, Nellie. And tell me, how's Joe? You're not working him too hard, are you?"

She smiled and replied: "No, it's not me who's driving him; it's this business. Seems to me he should take a leaf out of your book because from what I see, you're not working quite so hard yourself anymore. How have you been able to do it without your business suffering?"

The man smiled at her as if harbouring a secret. He knew those who knew him had noticed his building renovation business had really taken off lately. Then just as he was about to reply, Joe walked in.

"Hey, Pete, how are you, buddy?"

He walked up and shook the outstretched hand of his old friend.

"Absolutely terrific Joe," he boomed. "And I'm now even better for seeing the two of you."

Joe too was a little surprised by his exuberance. This certainly didn't sound like the Pete of old. He shot a quick glance at his wife and noticed that she was smiling.

"Pete was just about to tell me how much he won on the lottery, Joe," she added while she had the chance. She was anxious not to lose the chance to pursue the subject.

"I mean, it must have taken the lottery to be able to change your lifestyle and your business prospects so radically, mustn't it Pete?" she continued.

The big man rocked with laughter. Nellie looked carefully at him in search of clues; it was often said she was a good judge of character and she didn't want her "skill" to let her down now. What she saw was a man oozing self-confidence and contentment.

"No, it's nothing like that," he replied.

"The lottery involves an element of luck, but with me it all it took was a simple decision."

Joe and Nellie were stunned. They looked at their friend with a mixture of curiosity and disbelief.

"What do you mean 'a decision'?" Joe asked.

"Just that, Joe. You see, I woke up one day and decided something had to change. I just couldn't go on like I had been. I wanted to take back control of my business, my life, and my future. It was as simple as that."

He paused, gathered his thoughts, and then continued.

"Actually, it all began ages ago, when my cousin gave me a ticket to this seminar that was being held in the town hall. It was a business seminar that was being run by a famous Business Coach. Anyway, I went along and really enjoyed it. In fact, I learned so much in such a short space of time, I thought I was going to change the world. But the next morning I got up and despite my best efforts, the calls came in, people wanted to see me, and I got trapped in my old routine. I realize now, I was like most business people. I was stuck in a rut. Needless to say I soon forgot about most of the seminar and over time I became too busy to use anything I'd learned there."

Pete paused to gather his thoughts.

"To cut a long story short, several months later I arrived at a point where I simply decided I had to take control of my destiny. Something had to change. I was working long hours, never really saw my wife or kids, never got to go on a real holiday, and truthfully, I really wasn't making anywhere near as much money as I should have been.

"I remembered a guy I met at the seminar who was working with the Coach. He'd told me about himself and mentioned how he was in the same boat as I was in, at the start. And then, he told me how over time his life had changed. So, I did the only thing I could do, I got on the phone and called the Coach on the off-chance he would be able see me."

Just then the door opened and a lady came in to buy a loaf of bread. Fortunately, she was quick and left with the loaf tucked firmly under her arm.

"As I was saying," Pete continued, "he answered the phone and I didn't quite know what to say. You know how it is. I couldn't for the life of me explain why I'd actually phoned him. I had to say something, so I asked him about the possibility of becoming my Business Coach. He eventually agreed when he knew how serious I was and, as you can see, my life has changed."

Joe whistled softly under his breath.

"What did he show you, Pete? I mean, he must have given you some awesome business secrets."

"He certainly did, Joe. And I'm so grateful, I feel almost indebted to him, if you know what I mean. What he showed me was without doubt the most powerful stuff I have ever learned, but the way he put it made it really quite simple."

He steered them towards the counter as he spoke.

"Got a pen and paper? I want to show you something." "This is the secret to my success," Pete said as he drew. "Take a look at this simple diagram. It's the Coach's 6 Steps to Massive Results."

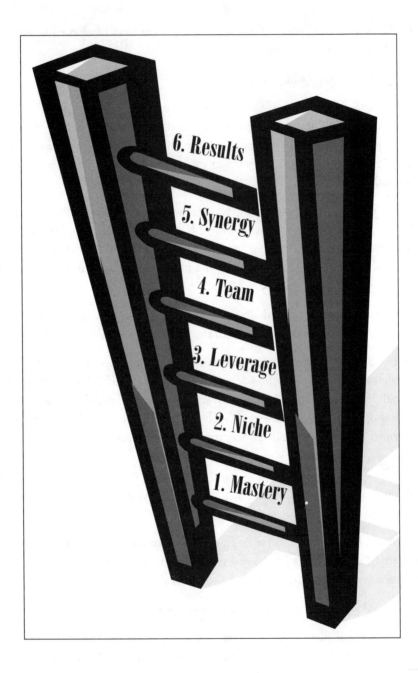

Joe and Nellie leaned closer.

"Looks simple enough, Pete, but what's it all mean?" Joe asked.

"It's called the 6 Steps Program and it's designed for every business," Pete continued.

"My Coach used this to walk me up the ladder of business growth, making sure I started with a solid base before getting into the serious growth. We started off at the bottom—at the *Mastery Level*—getting the fundamentals in place, so I could be certain of at least making a profit in my business. And as you probably know, that was a major thing for me because profit was really a bit of a hit and miss in my business."

"I know exactly what you mean; it's the same for us," Joe responded, shooting a quick glance at Nellie, who nodded.

"It was great, I mean, I had some of the stuff done, but my Coach helped me put it together in a way that made it all work and produce far greater results. I worked through the numbers to not only know the results, revenues, and profits, but also understand the Key Performance Indicators that led to them. The last thing my Coach wanted me to do was to wait until the end of the month, or even worse, the year, to see how I was doing. He wanted me to be able to know what to do to change those numbers along the way. The secret was simply testing and measuring."

Joe was impressed.

"Sounds very accountinglike, Pete. I mean, were you able to understand it first time around?"

"That's the funny thing, Joe. With my Coach it's dead easy and fun too. Just like playing a game. But let me finish."

"Once he got me making a consistent base profit, I moved onto the next level—*Niche*—where I began marketing and focusing on making more revenues at my new higher margin. We got this through repeat business and working my average dollar sale, right through to building a great sales team and pumping more new leads through my door."

"Sounds like you were moving ahead at a heck of a rate, Pete, what with a sales team and all that. You never had any of that before."

"That's true, but it gets better. At the *Leverage Level,* I learned how to have my business run like a well-oiled machine, whether I was there or not. For the first time in my life, I was able to get into golf in a big way. And boy has it done wonders for my game. You see, my business is working so well, I don't have to. Coach says sometimes *Leverage* is all many business owners need, but not me, I had to start at the bottom of the ladder."

It was now Nellie who jumped forward and spoke.

"That sounds like the type of business we need, Pete. Do you know how long it's been since Joe and I even had a day off, let alone a real holiday?"

"Well the good news is you can, Nellie. See, one of the most important keys to achieving amazing *Synergy* is the next step on my Coach's ladder, building a *Team,* and I learned all about how to do this. In fact, he taught me everything from leadership through to recruiting the right people. The result of all this is huge. I'm a changed man. I don't have to slave away to make a half decent living anymore, thanks to my Coach. I work when I want and I have more time to do what I really enjoy, even if that includes some work!"

Joe was excited by what he was feeling and so was Nellie. It was clear to them that their friend was so enthusiastic about his business now and it was a dramatic change from before. And, if it worked for him, then maybe it could work for them too. And besides, both they and their business could do with some revitalizing.

"Pete, do you think you could teach us some of the Coach's stuff so our bakery could take off? I mean, so that we could get the odd day off now and again?"

"Man, as much as I would love to, I've only just learned this stuff myself and I'd probably end up doing you more harm than good. You see, I'm no teacher. The Coach is the guru at this, not me."

Joe looked disappointed.

"Do you think I should give him a call then? Are you suggesting he should coach us too, just like he did you?"

Pete thought for a second.

"Don't know if he will. I mean he only takes on a certain number of clients at any one time. He told me as much when I first phoned him."

"But it would be worth a try, wouldn't it? I mean even if we were to go on a waiting list or something." "Can you give me your Coach's phone number, then?" Joe asked tentatively. "I'd like to see him to see if there's any hope for us, if you know what I mean."

"I guess you're right," Pete responded and began digging in his diary. "Here's his number. Make sure you tell him I referred you, as he likes to deal with friends of his existing clients."

Part 1

▌ Mastery

"Hard work never killed anyone," Joe spat as he pummelled his big fists simultaneously into the ball of dough on the bench in front of him. It was like this every morning and had been so for the past 20 years. The old clock on the far wall said it was going on 5:00 a.m. and he still had ten balls of dough to knead.

"What rubbish! This work is slowly killing me," he said. "And all for what?"

It's not that he hated his work. In fact, he loved it. But that's what was driving him crazy.

They came from miles around to buy his bread. He hated having to turn some of them away empty-handed, but he didn't know how he could do otherwise. He was already working long hours—he started preparing the ovens at 3:00 a.m. every day, he never got home much before 7:00 p.m., and no one could do it like he could. After all, he had tried employees, and most of them just created more work for Nellie and himself, not less.

Joe didn't know how he'd cope if Nellie, his long-suffering wife of 25 years, had gotten a job elsewhere. He was grateful for small mercies.

Joe swung his attention back to the task at hand; he knew he couldn't afford to let his mind wander. But he also knew that he couldn't go on like this much longer. He would be really happy if the Coach would take his business under his wing.

Joe continued kneading the dough, making sure to keep it moving by bringing it forward to the edge of the bench, turning it over delicately with the tips of his stubby fingers, and then pressing down into it with the balls of his hands. This he did over and over again—bringing it forward, pressing down and rolling it back—until the ball was nice and smooth.

He breathed in deeply and smiled as that wonderful aroma of baking bread filled his lungs.

"Yep, this is what keeps me going," he thought.

The life of a small business owner was monotonous for Joe. Yet he could still enjoy it, if only he could turn things around like Pete had been able to do.

He found himself on an emotional seesaw since he had phoned the Coach. One minute he was up in the clouds with anticipation and enthusiasm, and the next he was down in the dumps with self-doubt. After all, Pete was more astute than he was, or so he kept telling himself. Pete was a streetwise businessman who was always able to take the rough with the smooth. He had a built-in survival ability that Joe didn't think he had. Joe was best when the going got tough. He rolled up his sleeves and worked harder.

Joe found that as his first appointment with the Coach grew closer, he got more and more nervous—or was it apprehension? He didn't know or care. All he knew was that the suspense was killing him.

Before he knew it, Nellie popped her head into the bakery and said: "Joe, he's here. Come on out and meet him, will you?"

Joe straightened up, wiped his hands on his apron, and made his way to the front of the bakery.

The tall man smiled at him and extended his hand.

"A pleasure to meet you, Joe," he said.

Joe shook his hand and began telling him about his business challenges without waiting to be asked.

"The trouble is," he explained, "we work our butts off, yet we still can't seem to bake enough for our customers. And it's a thankless job because at the end of the day we barely earn enough to make it worthwhile."

The Coach spent an hour or so quizzing Joe and Nellie about their business, their goals, the reasons they went into business in the first place, and so much more. It was quite painful at times, especially when the Coach would ask about things they knew nothing about, but it made them think, "how much have we been missing?"

Finally, Joe asked if there was any hope for them to succeed like Pete had.

"Tell me first, if I agree to coach you, will you be what I call good clients? By this I mean, will you agree to work hard as we go along? You need to understand that I am going to be pushing you and I'll expect you to keep up with me. See, you'll be expected to put in all the hard work now, so you'll have the easy life later on. These are my rules, I don't coach just anybody—I only work with people who are serious about wanting to get ahead."

Joe's confidence disappeared rather quickly. He found himself at a loss for words and was embarrassed by the silence.

It was Nellie who saved the situation.

"Can you help us? Will you be our Coach?"

"I'm not sure. I need to know you are coachable. I need to be sure you have the passion for success, that you will do whatever it takes to achieve your goals. You see, I will expect you to be diligent, try all the suggestions I make, be willing to read all the books I recommend, implement all strategies you say you will, and pay your accounts on time. I am a hard taskmaster and I don't plan on wasting my time or yours. See, it's quite obvious to me that you need to change and that you want to change, but the question is do you 'have to' change?"

Joe looked over to Nellie, who nodded in agreement. The Coach opened his briefcase, pulled out a few files, and began going through the preparatory paperwork with them.

When the paperwork was complete, Joe sat back both relaxed and nervous; he wasn't sure if he should panic or celebrate.

It was the Coach who broke the silence, "OK, to get started we need to realize that you haven't quite come to grips with the Mastery Level of business yet," he replied.

Joe was a little taken aback. He hadn't expected the Coach to be so forthright.

"Tell me, what do you mean by *Mastery Level*?" he asked.

Joe surprised himself. It was the first time that anything to do with what he thought was the dry and boring world of business had actually sparked some interest. He normally left that side of things to Nellie.

"I'm glad you asked, Joe. I'll explain it to you as simply as I can. The first stage of growing any business is about making sure you deliver profitably, productively, and with enough information to make great decisions. That's what Mastery is."

Joe found himself enthralled and wanted to hear more. He had this feeling deep down inside that it had become imperative for them to learn more.

"Coach, I know it's going to be hard work, and I know the money we invest with you will make it tight at first, but I don't think we have a choice. We've got to do this and we've got to do it now," Joe blurted out. Nellie was just about in tears as she agreed.

The Coach smiled and nodded.

"Let's set a date for me to come around for an Alignment Consultation so we can get started. Is that OK with you?"

They agreed and decided on a time the following week.

"Can you explain briefly what this Alignment Consultation is, Coach, as we haven't done anything like this before?" Joe continued.

"Sure, Joe. It's nothing more than an opportunity for me to evaluate your business and personal goals, and to identify, in even more depth than we have today, the different areas of untapped potential in your business. Think of it as an in-depth look at your goals—both business and personal, and the sales, marketing, and business strategies you've used and what results you achieved. From that session, together we'll create a basic road map for the future of your business and our coaching."

Joe was impressed.

"Man, I feel as if we are beginning to make progress already, even though we haven't yet begun."

"Sure you have, Joe; you've completed the hardest part already and that's to make the decision to become responsible for your own future."

Later that evening Joe called Pete to let him know how his meeting with the Coach had gone.

"Man, he's tough, Pete," Joe began.

"You think that's tough! You haven't seen anything yet. Wait until you really start coaching. The one thing he taught me early on is that as long as you know where you're going, it's easy to get there. So what I suggest you do between now and the time you do your Alignment is to think long and hard about your goals. Jot down as many as you can—both business and private."

Joe took his friend's advice seriously and thanked him before hanging up. He reached for his notepad and began writing what the Coach had taught him that day.

Mastery—
The first stage of growing any
business is about making sure we
deliver profitably, productively, and
with enough information to make
great decisions.

Joe and Nellie had waited all day for the Coach to arrive. Joe was especially eager because the Alignment Consultation had put things into perspective for him. He hadn't realized before that his personal goals had actually been working against his business goals. It had suddenly become clear to him why he continually found himself being tugged between the bakery and his home. He never seemed to have time enough for both. Until then he had simply put that down to what being in business was all about. But now that the Coach had helped both him and Nellie align their personal and business goals, Joe found himself all fired up and really excited about learning how to get the full potential from his business.

Since the Alignment both Joe and Nellie had this zest for life and business; it was like they could now see the light at the end of the tunnel.

As the Coach had said, "Before we start coaching, we have to know where you are now, and have a very clear picture of where each step is taking us; only then can we draw a road map or plan."

They had even set goals for a holiday and for Joe to finally get a new car.

Joe blurted from the back room, "It's funny how we tried this goal setting ourselves in the past and it never really worked."

Nellie's reply was straight to the point, "I know, it was really great to have someone asking the questions; it helped me get very clear, very quickly, and boy did he ask a lot of questions."

They both felt a level of calmness, for just a moment, before they knew it was time to get back to work.

Even though their coaching session was scheduled for 3:00 p.m.—a time the shop was always quiet—they had to drag themselves through the early morning hours. Midday was always busy, and that occupied their impatient minds. The afternoon flew past, and before they knew it, Nellie was calling Joe.

"The Coach is here, Joe," she said with real excitement in her voice. "Better come quick as we don't want to keep him waiting."

She disappeared to the front of the shop and asked the Coach to follow her to their small office.

"Good to see you again, Coach," Joe said as he entered the office. "How have things been going?"

"Great," the Coach replied, as he pulled up a chair and made himself comfortable. "I'm really glad you've decided to take a proactive approach to your business. After mastering the basics, Joe, you'll find that it's all quite straightforward and easy to understand."

"I hope you're right," quipped Nellie. "If you knew Joe like I know him, you'd have some doubts. He may be good in the bakery, but when it comes to business..."

"That's fine, Nellie, most small business owners are in the same boat. They're really good at what they do—that's usually the main reason they went into business in the first place—but nobody ever taught them how to run a business. Do you understand the difference?"

The Coach paused and looked from Nellie to Joe.

"Are you comfortable with the difference, Joe?"

"Yeah, sure Coach, I see where you are coming from. I'm a baker and so for me baking is my trade, but all the business side of things, like tax and accounting, are things I've never bothered to learn. Usually, we leave that side of things to our accountant."

The Coach smiled.

"That's one of the challenges with small business, Joe. You see, most accountants are great at looking back into the past with your tax and accounting, but when it comes to planning ahead and running a business, there's so much more than just the numbers. You have to imagine that as a business owner you need to learn about all areas, and trust me we will get to them over time, but yes, Joe, the numbers are very important in this first stage, the stage I call Mastery."

Everyone was nodding, so the Coach went on.

"OK, it goes without saying that you're in business to make money," the Coach said as he leaned back in his chair. He wanted to begin gently because he could see that Joe and Nellie were looking a little stressed.

"My first job as your Business Coach is to make sure your business remains viable. That's my main concern. You see, what's the point of jumping straight in and designing clever marketing campaigns or developing expansion plans if the business isn't fundamentally sound to start with? The last thing we want to do is invite long-term challenges."

Nellie was still nodding in agreement. Joe seemed unmoved.

"Having said that, my main task at this stage is to find out how well you are managing your resources, and by this I mean your time and money."

The Coach paused for a while so that what he had just said had time to sink in.

"We'll start by concentrating on the money first. I need to find out just how well you are in control of your financial situation. Then I'm going to teach you how to understand your books, and for that matter, how to keep the right books in the first place."

This was clearly Nellie's area.

"Yes, I think I know about that, Coach," she replied. "I may not have an accounting qualification, but I know enough to be able to keep our books up-to-date. Our accountant has never complained and we haven't had any major blues over the years. Well, not on account of the books, that is."

The Coach nodded.

"That's great, Nellie. In fact, that gives you a huge advantage because I won't have to spend time going over the basics like how to read a Balance Sheet, for instance. But do you understand what the numbers are telling you, what ratios to work with, and how you can manage your business based on the numbers?"

"I've always thought I knew, Coach, but I suppose I'm about to find out I've got some more to learn."

"Probably, Nellie, and you'll get to see things in a completely new light." The Coach could see that she was taking an interest in what he was saying. She shot a quick glance over to Joe and her heart sank; she could tell that he wasn't at all clear on what was being discussed.

The Coach had picked up on it as well, so he made a quick note for both Joe and Nellie.

Money Mastery—
Not only do I need to know my
historic numbers, but the ones that
will create my future as well.

"Money Mastery is a fascinating subject, and to master it you need to master each of the four most important areas of money in your business. Money Mastery consists of four subtopics—Break Even Mastery, Profit Margin Mastery, Reporting Mastery, and Test and Measure Mastery. Over the next few weeks, we're going work through each one in turn."

Joe began taking an interest now and jumped in before Nellie had a chance to speak.

"That's one phrase I've heard a lot about, Coach. For years I've always had to check up to make sure we break even. So I understand what it means, but I'd like to see your perspective on it."

Nellie began shuffling uncomfortably in her chair. The Coach guessed that she had been the one who had been constantly reminding Joe of the need to break even. It had probably become something of a sore point, he thought. Joe watched through the corner of his eye as the Coach pulled out a sheet of paper with a note on it.

Break-Even Mastery—
Know how many sales, customers, or
dollars I need to make per day to
break even, and then to hit my
profit goals.

"Nellie is quite right to have been pushing the issue, Joe. You see, unless you first concentrate on breaking even, you won't have a business to spend your time, money, or talents on growing."

"So how do we know simply whether we're breaking even, Coach?" Joe asked. "I mean, how can we tell quickly, without having to wait for our accountant to tell us each month?"

"That's a very good question, Joe," the Coach replied. "And it's an easy one to answer." "What are your fixed costs, Nellie?" the Coach asked.

"On average $4000 a week," she replied. "That's our rent, electricity, water, wages, and the cost of all our basic materials like flour."

"What about any marketing costs?" the Coach asked.

"We don't do anything like that regularly, Coach," she replied.

"OK, so if you are making, on average, $5 per sale, then you would need to make 800 sales each week to break even. Can you follow that? 800 times 5 equals 4000."

Joe felt a whole lot easier already, and it showed. He was sitting back more comfortably in his chair and the frown had disappeared from his forehead.

"I think I am going to enjoy this, Coach. You make it look so simple."

"It really is simple, Joe," the Coach replied. "You'll see, you'll get the hang of it really quickly, and when you understand the underlying principles and begin applying some of the techniques and strategies I'll be giving you, your business will really begin to fly."

It was Nellie who spoke next.

"I guess the next thing you'll be asking us, Coach, is if we know what our actual exact break even figure is."

"You're on the ball, Nellie. That's exactly right and it's my guess you don't, because that's been my experience working with small business owners. Am I right?"

She nodded.

"What I want you to do between now and my next visit, which will be this time next week, if that's OK, is to work out your gross margin. And because you already know your approximate fixed costs, you can then work out your break-even point. Can you do that?"

"No worries, Coach. Consider it done," she responded.

"OK, folks, I'm going to leave you to it. When we get together next week I'm going to start off discussing Profit Margin Mastery. See you then."

For the first time in years Joe felt as if he was getting somewhere and things were changing. No longer did he feel as if he was merely going through the same motions—he knew that both he and Nellie were, for the first time in their lives, being proactive in running their business. It was only the beginning, but as the Coach had pointed out, getting started is the hardest part.

He couldn't wait for the Coach's next visit. He found himself itching to learn more. And this surprised him because he was never a good scholar.

"Coach, so good to see you," Joe said, as he showed his new business Coach into his office. He had felt like a small child on Christmas morning in the hours before the Coach arrived.

"Hi, Nellie," the Coach said as he pulled up his chair. "and how did it go with your homework?"

"Great, Coach, and I not only had fun collecting the data, but I also learned a few things. Turns out our break even point is 909 sales per week, or 152 per day for the 6 days we're open, because on average we only make $4.40 a sale. I really didn't know that our break-even point was as high as it's turned out to be."

"That's usually the case, Nellie, and it's one of the reasons so many small businesses go to the wall each year. They simply underestimate how much profit they need to make to stay viable. And speaking of profit, that's what we'll be looking at today."

"Now we're talking, Coach," Joe continued. "Profit is what I like, but hard as I may work, it doesn't seem to make a difference in how much profit we make."

Joe was clearly in his element now and he had usurped Nellie's traditional role as custodian of the bakery's finances.

"There's a very good reason for that, Joe," the Coach responded. "You see, contrary to how it appears, profit has nothing to do with the amount of time you put in. But I'm happy to see you're so passionate about making a profit, because that's really the key figure a business should be measured on. Understand that being successful in business has very little to do with the size of your business or what its revenues are. It's all about how much profit you make; for a company to stay in business, keep employing people, and keep doing good work, there has to be a profit."

Joe was listening intently. And so was Nellie.

"If there's one thing I want you to remember from today's coaching session, it's this: In business, Profit is King."

Nellie picked up her pencil and began writing what the Coach told her next.

Profit Margin Mastery—
I can set a budget for profit each day,
week, or month, and implement
strategies to get there.

Joe and Nellie found themselves immersed in the discussion and interacting with their Coach as they would never have believed possible. They talked about how, once they had an accurate handle on their break-even amount for each month and how much profit each of their products made, they could then very simply work out how much they need to sell each month just to break even and then to reach their profit goals. They found the discussion extremely stimulating because it related directly to their very own business and not to some hypothetical one. And they were able to understand.

"You know, Coach, we never really set profit goals, we kind of talked about it, but it was never budgeted for and even worse, we never developed a plan for it," said Nellie with some excitement.

"That's usually because most people don't know how to make their goals real, especially in business, so they find it easier NOT to set goals. But, now it's time to get to the fun part," the Coach continued.

"You mean what we have just been discussing wasn't fun?" Joe quipped. "You could've fooled me."

"No, not when you see what we'll be talking about next," the Coach replied. "We're now going to put in place measures to increase the profit you make. We're going to be doing things that will earn you more money."

"Now you're talking, Coach," Nellie said, "That's something we really need, don't we, Joe?"

Joe nodded.

"One of the most common questions I get asked by business owners from all over the world is how they can improve their profits," the Coach continued.

"Profit is the one thing they all want more of. And that's understandable, because PROFIT is the very thing we should be in business for. Back in 1908, they summed it up well when a unionist said, 'the worst crime against working people is a company that fails to operate at a profit.' And, I'd have to agree."

They nodded.

"Anyway, my answer to these business owners is simple, and it always comes as something of a surprise. I always tell them that profit is the one thing they can't directly get more of." Joe looked stunned.

"Run that past me one more time will you, Coach?"

"Profit is something business owners simply can't get more of—directly. But they certainly can influence their bottom lines by working on, and improving, the variables that contribute towards the profitability of their business. Do you see what I'm getting at?"

Both Joe and Nellie were now confused.

"You should view your business in terms of its five separate, distinct areas," the Coach began explaining. "You need to break your business down into a simple formula of what the business looks like. It doesn't matter where you are, what you do, or how big your business is, this formula still applies.

"I call it the *Business Chassis*. When you truly understand how a business works, you'll realize that profit is a factor that's the result of other variables and can't be directly altered in isolation. The same applies for customers and revenue."

They sat quietly and listened.

"So what exactly is the Business Chassis, Coach?" Joe asked.

"Think of it as a formula."

The Coach pulled a sheet from his briefcase and handed it to the couple.

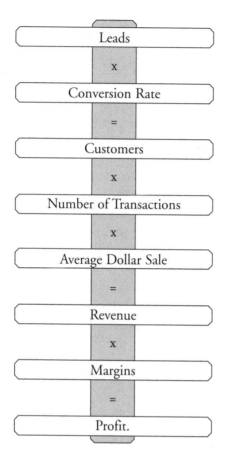

"You can't get more customers. But you can increase the number of leads you get and improve your conversion rate, which together will result in more customers. Similarly, you can't get higher revenues without improving the number of transactions each customer makes, as well as the average amount of dollars they spend."

Nellie was first to respond.

"I'm beginning to see what you're getting at, very clever Coach. But don't let me stop you now."

The Coach nodded.

"Think of it this way: if you always baked chocolate cakes, Nellie, but now wanted to bake a fruit cake, you wouldn't continue to use the recipe for the chocolate cake, would you?"

"Of course not, Coach, I'd use the recipe for a fruit cake!"

"That's right, because if you didn't, what would you end up with? Another chocolate cake. It's the same with business.

"Profit has to do with the last part of the Business Chassis—the Margins. Activities designed to improve Margins have a direct effect on Profit. They involve things like pricing policy, discounting, up-selling, and controlling expenditure, and I'm sure you are familiar with these, at least in general terms."

Nellie nodded.

"But there are other, less obvious, activities that are just as important. Things like stock management, accounts management, time management, and even your ability to know your numbers, to mention but a few. But first, I want you to set what I call your profit break-even point. This will guide the decisions you take here."

"Do you want us to set our profit budget now, Coach?" Nellie asked.

"Yes, how much profit do you budget for at present?"

"Well, we don't budget for anything specific, Coach," she replied. "We kind of just do the best we can."

"Then how much would you like to make each month?" the Coach probed.

They thought for a moment, thinking back over their past performances.

"Let's say $10,000 a month, Coach. How does that sound?" Nellie continued.

"That's fantastic, and it's also reasonable given the size of your company. Now what does that mean as far as the number of sales you need to make each day, week, and month?"

Nellie had begun hitting the buttons of her calculator even before the Coach had finished speaking. Then she jotted down numbers on her pad of paper.

"Looks like we will need to make 1477 sales a week at $4.40 each to achieve our new weekly target of $6500. This will give us our $10,000 profit a month profit, Coach. That means we must aim at making 246 sales a day and not the 152 we make currently."

Joe gulped, "Coach, I really don't think I can bake that much extra without some help."

"What you have to remember, Joe, is that Coaching is about getting there with a plan. It's great to set the goal, like we just have, but now we have to work out how to get there."

The Coach paused for a drink of water, and then continued.

"There's another basic concept I want to go over with you both before I forget. What is the difference between 'margin' and 'markup'?"

A long silence followed. Neither Joe nor Nellie were keen to venture a guess.

"Think of it this way: your margin is a percentage of your *selling* price, whereas your markup is a percentage of your *cost* price. Get it?"

Joe and Nellie both nodded as the Coach continued. "But there's something else you need to bear in mind when working on your profit and that can be seen if you look at the last part of the business chassis: Revenues x Margin = Profit. So to really get an accurate understanding of what you need to do each week to meet your profit target, you need to know what your margins are.

"You've just worked out how much you need to sell each week. That gives you your revenue and sales goal, so you now need to work backwards to find the margin you have now and your goal margin to hit your budgeted figure of $10,000 a month profit. Is that clear?"

Joe had learned an awful lot that day, probably more than he had ever learned before about running a business. And he had enjoyed it immensely.

"To finish up then, folks, I want you to think about what you have learned today and how you can apply it to your bakery. Our immediate aim is to come up with a handful of strategies that will increase your profit and in so doing, ensure that your business becomes healthy and profitable. You could, for instance, simply increase your prices by 5 percent across the board or you could stop offering discounts. You could also make it easy for your customers to buy by accepting credit cards and debit cards and also negotiating the rates on the cards that you currently accept. And what about joining a small business buying group to get some of your supplies at a larger discount?"

Joe was enjoying it. He hadn't thought about business as really anything more than the work he did baking. Sure, he knew there was more to it, but who had the time to learn?

"So just before I go, are there any questions? Are you clear on what you have to do between now and this time next week?"

Joe felt the past few weeks had really flown by. Work hadn't seemed quite so boring. He found himself thinking about what the Coach had said, and it made the time he spent in the bakery so much more meaningful. Each time he took a fresh loaf of bread from the oven he saw it in terms of profit. Each and every loaf he baked contributed to the bottom line of the business.

Over the last few weeks together with the Coach, they had implemented several very simple, yet powerful, Margin boosting ideas and they were really starting to take shape. A couple of ideas had flopped, but most had worked well, and of course there was still a lot to learn.

Joe was honest, though. After years in business, it was now Profit that interested him most. He suspected that Reporting Mastery, the topic of their next coaching session, would be of more interest to Nellie than to him. He knew he wasn't looking forward to it as he greeted the Coach that afternoon.

"Before we get down to discussing various strategies you've used to start boosting your profits," the Coach commenced, "there's one very important concept I need to discuss, and that's knowing where your business is *before* you start massively implementing anything. I want you to write down what I am about to say."

Joe was right. Nellie was clearly the one more interested in this topic. She slid him a piece of paper on which she had jotted what the Coach had dictated.

Reporting Mastery—
It's vital to know my numbers each
day, week, and month so I can make
decisions for the future.

"You need to know what the situation is before you attempt to change it. Otherwise, you'll have no idea whether you've successfully implemented change or not, and if you have, by how much," the Coach continued.

Nellie was sitting on the edge of her chair and taking in every word the Coach uttered.

"Understand this: if you want to get to a particular destination, you'll never know how to get there unless you know where you started. Make sense?"

Nellie nodded.

"For instance, if you want to increase your profitability by 25 percent more than it is now, what does that actually mean? It's meaningless unless you know what your profitability was to start with."

Nellie was still nodding.

"Before we get too far into implementing your profit-boosting strategies, we need to conduct two surveys, one to determine exactly what your Average Dollar Sale is now, and the other to determine what your Margins are. We've already talked about this, so you should already know basically what these figures are, shouldn't you, Nellie?"

She just kept on nodding. Joe noticed and smiled.

"Our average dollar sale is about $4.40," she said.

"Congratulations—you're already something of a rarity in the small business community," the Coach said with a smile. "I'm sure you're familiar with the term stocktaking. Most businesses conduct them regularly because it's a requirement, from an accounting point of view. But how many take stock of other areas of their operation? Why should you confine stocktaking to that part of your business that deals predominantly with stock?"

The Coach paused to let what he had just said sink in.

"You see, you should be 'taking stock' of where your business is, as far as all your marketing and business growth efforts are concerned. You need to know where you stand at any particular point in time."

Nellie jumped in and said: "But what if we don't do any marketing, Coach?"

"Don't only think about advertising as marketing, Nellie. It's more diverse than that. But we'll get to that later. For now, I want you to think about how you know where you stand at the moment."

Now it was Joe's turn to jump in.

"I know we can't really count it like we do our stock, but there must be a way we can *measure* it, Coach. I think what you're getting at is what we just did with our margins and overheads. Would that be right?"

"Exactly right, Joe. And when it comes to marketing, you can *test* to see which elements are working and which are not. That's why I refer to this activity as *Testing and Measuring*. It's just another way of taking stock and recording your Key Performance Indicators or KPIs. More on this later team."

Joe was surprised that he wasn't as bored with this session as he had suspected he would be.

The Coach handed each of them a piece of paper and said: "OK, so let's get practical. We're now going to exactly remeasure your *Average Dollar Sale*. Getting a handle on your Average Dollar Sale is not that difficult to do. In fact, it's dead simple. What I want you to do over the next week is to make a note of every sale you make. You can keep it at the cash register if you like, but whatever happens it must be filled in after each and every sale. Then at the end of the week, you do the calculation to find out how much each customer spends, on average, every time she buys from you. Got it?"

Nellie nodded and said: "So we just divide by the total number of customers to work out the average, Coach?"

"Exactly, and I know we already have an estimate of this number, but in business it's about growing the numbers and how will we know if we've grown it if we don't keep testing and measuring" he replied.

The Coach gave them another piece of paper. "And, Nellie, here you'll see where we measure your Margins each and every day. It's a simple tool that will show the days when you sell more high-margin items and more low-margin items.

"Once you've completed these simple surveys, you'll have an excellent idea of the Average Dollar Sale and your current Margins. That gives us more information to make decisions with and we'll know what we have to improve on, or if we've started to make improvements already. You'll have a benchmark against which to measure the strategies we've been putting into place. And by Testing and Measuring you'll know when you've reached your objective, by how much you've improved, and the cost-effectiveness of the strategies. You'll also have a direct and accurate way of seeing the effect these strategies have on your bottom line."

Joe was warming to the subject.

"You know, this Reporting Mastery is interesting after all, Coach."

"I never said it wasn't, Joe. I'm sure you'll discover that business is interesting once you see it the way I do.

"There are a few basic tools that you need to understand. These are all part of Reporting Mastery," the Coach continued.

"Nellie, I guess you are familiar with Profit and Loss Statements, Cashflow Statements, and Balance Sheets?"

She thought for a while before replying.

"Only basically, Coach. I leave most of that to our accountant."

"What do you understand about them, Joe?" the Coach responded.

"Gee, Coach, you're talking to the wrong person. I work with the dough, not the money, remember."

"Try it, Joe. Tell me what you understand when you see these words."

Joe thought for a moment and then said: "I guess the Profit and Loss Statements let us know whether we are making a profit or a loss for the month or whatever period it covers. The Cashflow Statement probably shows us what our cashflow situation is like—you know, do we have more outstanding than we have in the bank, and the Balance Sheet, I think shows the state of our business at any point in time."

"Very good, Joe, you've got it. See, it's really quite simple. Problem is most people over complicate it. Now, remember to carry out the survey we talked about, because it'll give you a good insight into our next topic, which is Testing and Measuring, and to go back to our profit strategies to see how they're doing."

"What exactly do you mean when you say Testing and Measuring, Coach?" Joe asked with renewed confidence.

"It's very simple, Joe. We test new strategies on a small scale to find out whether they will work before implementing them on a larger scale. We also test and measure to find out where your business is, before we work on growing it. This means that we'll be able to see whether we've succeeded (or not) after we've implemented the strategies and systems. But more on that soon. In the meantime, I want you to begin thinking about hiring a bookkeeper to get all these reports out on a regular basis. I'll see you both next week."

It was several weeks later that they moved onto the next *Money Mastery* subject, as both Joe and Nellie took a while to get their homework done, but at least now their bookkeeper had the reports out each month, and their Coach had shown them how to read each one, so they were able to make intelligent and informed decisions.

Joe was first to pipe up this week, "You know, Coach, we've come a long way in just a few short weeks, but what amazes me most is that our Margins and our Average Dollar Sale seem to be already growing and we haven't really used many strategies yet."

"That's true, Joe. Just by focusing we can get a small growth in each area and it all multiplies together to get a great result on the bottom line. Testing and Measuring is also powerful stuff. Remember, you cannot manage what you do not measure, and we need to know if these numbers have increased or just seem to have increased," said the Coach with a level of pride in his students' work.

"With that, we come now to the final part of *Money Mastery*," said the Coach as he continued the week's coaching session. "You'll recall that we've already covered *Break Even Mastery*—where we worked out how many customers per week you need to break even, *Profit Margin Mastery*—where we worked out how many customers and what average dollar sale per day you need to hit your profit goals, as well as putting into practice some new ideas to get profit moving, and *Reporting Mastery*—where we found out where we are now, so we know how far we have to go. All we now have to do is continue our *Test and Measure Mastery* to complete the first Mastery category. By the way, can you remember what the other major Mastery categories are?"

Joe and Nellie sat there scratching their heads and tried to come up with the answer the Coach was looking for.

"Let's see," Joe muttered. "What we've been discussing is all part of Money Mastery. That means mastering the money in our business. What else do we need to master?"

The Coach interrupted to give him a pointer.

"Remember, we're only looking at the survival stage of the business here and nothing else. Only mastering the basics so the business can become fundamentally healthy and viable."

Joe thought for a while and then said: "I have a feeling you mentioned it right at the beginning, during our first coaching session. Let me think. What is another main challenge we face? Ah, it would have to be time because we never seem to have enough of it. Time Mastery—that would be one, Coach."

"Very good, Joe. Now what about the third?" he asked, looking at Nellie.

"I haven't mentioned this one before, but it ranks alongside time and money as being a most important area of business that must be mastered in order to ensure the survival of the business."

Nellie looked thoughtfully across the desk to the Coach, but her mind remained blank.

"No, it's no use, Coach. Put us out of our misery, will you?" she said.

"It's Delivery Mastery. You have to have a means of reliably and efficiently delivering what you make or sell to your target market. But we'll look at that in more detail in a few weeks. Right now we are going to walk through Test and Measure Mastery."

Nellie flipped over to a clean page in her trusty notebook and wrote as the Coach spoke:

Test and Measure Mastery—
I can predict my future profits by measuring the Key Performance Indicators in my business—KPIs.

Joe leaned back and stretched in his chair, then yawned loudly, oblivious to the slight disruption he had caused. The Coach didn't mind because he was looking for a natural break at this point, he wanted this next session to sink in well.

"Let me start by saying that testing and measuring is vital for any business, as you've already started to see. If you're not testing and measuring everything you do, you won't know what's working and what's not. You won't know which marketing strategies to keep running, which to drop, and which to give more time to because they're showing promising signs."

Joe was warming to the subject.

"This means you should be doing two things when implementing profit or sales boosting strategies: you need to know what your numbers are *before* the strategies are started, and then you need to test and measure the results of your strategies *as you go along*. That way you can refine, hone, redirect or cancel strategies before they cost you lots of money and have the opposite effect to what you originally wanted."

Joe looked across to Nellie and said: "See, I knew we should have been doing something to see if that ad campaign we ran in the paper last Easter was worth it."

"But what could we have done—ask everyone that came in to buy? Don't be stupid. Where would we have got the time?" she replied.

"That's at the very heart of what we're now doing, Nellie. Freeing up time and money so you can do this vital testing and measuring. And yes, you often do have to literally ask everyone where they heard about your special or whatever; other times we make special offers so you know which advertisement a customer comes in from," the Coach responded. "But don't worry too much about that right now because we'll be getting into more detail over the next few weeks."

Nellie sat back and Joe clearly felt he had been let off the hook.

"So what did you discover about your average dollar sale?" he continued.

Nellie gathered her survey forms and tally sheet.

"It turns out our average dollar sale is only $3.75 at the moment, Coach," she responded.

"What did you think about that?" he asked.

"It came as something of a shock, I can tell you," Joe chipped in. "We thought the $4.40 from that one day we first measured it was right, but it turns out Saturday is higher than the rest of the week."

"Shortly, you'll decide which of the powerful profit-building strategies we'll continue with and once we get to *Niche*, we'll start on more *Average Dollar Sale* strategies. So far we've started off with just five strategies because that's going to make it easier for you to test and measure the results."

Now it was Nellie who spoke.

"Can you give us some idea of the process involved when doing this, Coach? I mean, because we've never done anything like this before, we don't even know the basics."

The Coach thought for a moment and then continued.

"Sure, Nellie. That's what coaching is all about. So here's what to do: Once you've set in place your chosen strategies, you redesign the *Testing and Measuring Sheets* to monitor the results. Then prune, modify, and increase. Test and measure for another two weeks. Check your strategies. Be honest with yourself. Are you cutting corners or being diligent? Now branch out and implement some of the other new strategies you'll have chosen but didn't implement at first. Do one at a time and track the results by repeating the steps I've just mentioned. Compare the results you get."

Nellie was meticulously taking notes while the Coach spoke. She knew she was the person who would be responsible for this area of the business.

"If you're not getting the results you want, try another *Margin* strategy or two. But don't be disheartened. You may need to try a few before you reach the results you're after. You see, every industry is different: what works well for one might not work for another. Some businesses may not deal directly with the buying public, making certain strategies irrelevant, although most can be adapted to suit any situation."

"You may find that more than one strategy needs to be implemented simultaneously. If so, that's fine. Very often, five or six profit-increasing strategies together produce a compound effect that sends the bottom line rocketing."

"But don't persist with something that isn't working, just because you happen to *like* one particular strategy or because you think it *should* work. If at first it doesn't work, give it another try, then another. But after that, if you still see negative or inconclusive results, then drop it."

Nellie was pleased with herself, as she had understood everything that was discussed. What's more, it actually made sense. She could see the rationale behind testing and measuring, and it all began falling into place.

The Coach pulled another few spreadsheets from his briefcase and proceeded to show each of them to Joe and Nellie, "So, now that you've made good progress on measuring your average dollar sale and margins, it's time to add the three other areas of the Business Chassis to your measuring homework. Do you remember the other three?"

Joe was in with the first two, "the number of prospects and the conversion rate, Coach."

"Great Joe, *Number of Leads* and *Conversion Rate* and the other one?"

Nellie stammered, "It was repeat business, I think, Coach, I can't remember what you called it though."

"That's correct, Nellie. It's here on your sheet, the *Number of Transactions*. Now over the next few weeks we need to get a good picture of how many new people come into the shop or call for orders, how many of them actually buy, and how often they come back," the Coach explained.

"Coach, is there an easy way to do that? I mean, how do we know how often people buy from us without spending our whole day working it out?" was Nellie's reply.

"You're right, Nellie. This can be very time-consuming if you let it, but the magic of the Chassis is that when we know most of the other easy numbers, we can work back to find out how often your customers come in. Let's just get it started and what we'll find is that it all falls into place," said the Coach, trying to give Nellie the confidence not to panic about it being perfectly accurate at the start.

"Well folks, we've made good progress today. Go home and digest what we have discussed so far, because once we've got this right we can move onto Delivery Mastery. And by the way, from here on in I will be coaching you over the phone because that's the most effective way there is. You do have a speaker phone, don't you?"

Nellie nodded, then replied: "But, Coach, won't it be better that we still meet this way? I mean it's so much more personal."

"That's right, it's more personal, but my goal is to teach you how to run your business over the phone from anywhere in the world. This way you get to see it firsthand."

He paused to let them get a feeling for what he had just said and then continued.

"Also, it really is better over the phone because you have to concentrate that much more and there's less chance you'll get distracted. It's also more efficient, so you will be able to get back to running your business that much sooner. Trust me; you'll soon see what I mean. Call me at 3:00 sharp."

That night Joe and Nellie went out for dinner. They had much to celebrate. They didn't go anywhere flashy, because that wasn't their style; they just went down to their local McDonald's.

They grabbed a table near the window because Joe liked to watch the passing parade. He knew most people in town, not only through the bakery, but also because he had lived there all his life.

The window seats also provided a little privacy, in a manner of speaking. While they provided an excellent window to the outside world, they were more secluded on the inside, which meant diners weren't as likely to be easily joined by others inside. Joe liked it that way because he valued what little private time he had with his wife.

So he was a little surprised when he felt a tap on the shoulder, just as he was about to tuck into his meal.

"Hi, Joe," the familiar voice boomed.

He swung around and was delighted to see it was Pete, his friend of old.

"Hi, Pete. You're just the person I need to see."

"Well, actually I'm alone, and wouldn't mind joining you two, if that's OK with you."

It was Nellie who beckoned to the empty chair at their table.

"So how's it going with the Coach?" Pete asked as he sat down.

"Man, you weren't wrong when you said he would work us," Joe replied.

"I really didn't know just how much we didn't know about business," he said.

Pete nodded thoughtfully.

"So that means you must still be at the *Mastery Level.* Have you started testing and measuring profit strategies to build your *Margins* yet?"

Nellie was surprised.

"Funny you should mention that, Pete. We've just been talking about that and it's something we would like to bounce off you, if that's OK."

"Sure, Nellie. What worked straight off for me was probably the simplest strategy anyone could use. I increased my prices by 10 percent across the board."

Joe straightened up in his chair.

"Didn't you lose business as a result, Pete?"

"No, not at all. You know it's a funny thing, but I reckon I was my own problem here because that was exactly my thoughts before I did it. But you know what? Very few people seemed to notice—or care. Actually, come to think of it a few people did complain, but they used to complain about things anyway. And the Coach helped me through it, of course, but essentially it was a case of business as usual. On second thought, it wasn't as usual—I made a lot more profit."

Joe whistled in surprise.

"But think of some other things you could do, Joe, because the Coach will want you to test and measure at least five."

Joe thought for a moment and then said: "You know, when I was placing my order a few moments ago, the youngster at the counter asked me whether I wanted fries with my order. I said yes, even though I didn't really. It did occur to me that I had just bought something I hadn't originally intended buying."

"That's very perceptive of you, Joe. The Coach calls that up-selling, and it's a great profit-generating strategy. Add that to your list."

It was Nellie's turn to speak now.

"That reminds me of the Green Grocer who always gives me a *big* shopping bag when I enter the store. And come to think of it, I always seem to fill it before I check out. What about that for a strategy, Joe?"

"I like it, Nellie. Let's add that to the list."

Pete jumped in just then and said: "Don't forget to stock high-margin goods. You know, just like the Ice Cream Shop does. That's great for your bottom line. And then there's also the whole subject of managing what you throw away. That can significantly rev up your profitability."

Joe was very pleased with what they had achieved that evening. Business was becoming fun, and he had even more ideas to test and measure.

"Do you know what the best thing about business is, Joe?" Pete asked. "It's that you really don't have to be brilliant to be a successful business owner. I've come to realize that far too many business owners look for rocket science, when the reality is that the business just has to be simple and systematic. See, what the Coach teaches us is that the small changes can add up to big results."

Again several weeks had passed as Joe and Nellie tried new ideas to boost their Margins. They tested on a small scale and then rolled out the strategies that worked. Of course, they spoke to the Coach every week, sometimes even more often, especially as Nellie got further into the measuring of her KPIs.

Her excitement was clear as she actually started to see how growing their business would happen over time. Joe was busy baking his higher-margin stock and really was focused on getting more profits in the door. They were working longer hours, but they knew where they were going and that meant a lot.

Of course, the Coach had kept them on track each week and when the Coach thought they were well on track with *Money Mastery*, it was time to move onto *Delivery Mastery*.

Joe had always wondered about whether he could do more when it came to delivering his products to his many customers. But that's as far as he got because every time he and Nellie had tried to discuss it, they always ran out of time even before they started. They knew they didn't want to get into the home delivery business and so that always seemed to end their discussion.

There appeared to be nothing to discuss.

So it was with more than a little interest that Nellie made this week's call at the time when the Coach had said they should. Not only did they want to show the Coach their results, but also they were dying to discover how relevant *Delivery Mastery* would be for them.

"Good afternoon, folks. Can you hear me OK?" the Coach began.

"Yes, you're coming through loud and clear, Coach."

"What we are going to discuss today is *Delivery Mastery*. We're going to look at what you're currently doing to manage and plan how you deliver the products you make for your customers. Did you receive my fax?"

Joe was holding it in his hands as he spoke.

Delivery Mastery—Consistency is more important than brilliance. Stop any leaks, as there is no use in filling the tub if the plug is left out.

"Yes, we did, Coach, but we don't deliver to our customers; they come to us," Joe interjected. There was no hint of stubbornness in his voice, just curiosity.

"You still have to deliver your product or service just like every other business. I think you've misunderstood what I mean by delivery. Think of it this way: you must make sure you deliver to your customers the products and services that they want. You need to be able to consistently deliver the right quality stock at the right time, at the right margin."

Joe nodded and said: "Oh, I can see what you are getting at, Coach. It's not about taking it to them; it's about making sure we deliver on our promise."

"That's right, Joe. It all boils down to planning, basic quality control, and tracking."

"Pardon?" Nellie replied.

"What I'm talking about here, Nellie, is planning your stock so you can ensure you have very few overruns—you know, so you don't bake heaps more than you know you'll sell. With service-type businesses, this would mean rostering on enough team members so that you can handle all the customers you expect will come in every day."

"Ah, I get it, Coach," Nellie replied.

"Planning stock also means making sure you can deliver what is already selling well. But there's more to it than that. It's also about concentrating on quality to ensure that the people who do business with you will come back. Understand that when we're talking about quality, I'm not suggesting that it's the level of quality that will create raving fans; all I'm saying is that your quality needs to be such that it doesn't make people run away."

"I get where you are coming from, Coach," she responded, and looked a little embarrassed.

"See Nellie, last week I went to a restaurant and they couldn't even get my order right. Marketing would be no use for them when they don't even have their basic Delivery Mastery in place," the Coach explained.

Joe had been thinking while this exchange had been going on.

"So, what you're saying, Coach, is we need to make sure our products are of enough quality to keep our customers, and we need to plan so we always have enough to serve all our customers what they want, when they want it," Joe summarized.

"That's it, Joe. Remember back to just last week when you told me you ran out of grain bread midmorning, and about how several weeks ago when that business with the big order came back because you'd given them some wrong bread rolls?" the Coach painfully pointed out.

"Well, those sort of mistakes can cost you dearly, and when you get more employees and more customers, the small mistakes that you can quickly cover now with good service and a real smile will become dam breakers—if that makes sense," the Coach kept going.

"So, here's your homework: list the top 5 to 10 customer complaint areas. You can have more if you need to, and then next week we'll discuss your ideas on how to solve each of them."

After the phone line went dead, Joe leaned back in his chair, looked at Nellie thoughtfully, and said: "Phew, that was quite a painful session, wasn't it? I reckon we got more than we bargained for this week, don't you?"

"You're not wrong there, Joe. I think we have our work cut out for us."

The speaker phone crackled into life. Joe and Nellie sat expectantly in their office. They'd worked hard over the last few weeks with the Coach to get their *Delivery* consistent, their quality consistent, and they'd even started using a new system to manage their production.

Now, not only were their margins better, but they'd removed most of the basic customer complaints, and delivery was running smoothly.

"So Coach, have we passed the test? Are we ready to move on?" asked Joe, waiting to hear what pearls the Coach had in store for them today. All they knew was that the next topic of discussion was to be *Time Mastery*. The Coach had sent them a short fax the day before that gave them the clue.

Time Mastery—
My productivity and the productivity of my people will determine my success and profitability.

Nellie was looking forward to being able to improve her use of time because they had both long since identified this as one of their greatest shortcomings. There never seemed to be enough time in the day to do all the things that needed doing. Joe had been complaining for years that he felt more like a slave to the bakery than the owner. This had taken all the fun out of working as far as he was concerned.

Nellie felt the same way. She couldn't remember the last time she went home without having to take a load of paperwork with her. There was always so much to do and what with having to serve customers and run errands as well, she simply didn't have the time during office hours to even think about doing it there. And then once she had seen to the dinner and all the other household duties, she was dead tired and just flopped into bed, exhausted every night. She knew she couldn't very well ask Joe for help because he started his day at 3:00 a.m. and needed all the sleep he could get.

There was no doubt about it; time was one of their greatest challenges.

"Good morning, folks. Joe, it's time to move on. I think you are moving well with both your *Money* and *Delivery Mastery*. What we're going to discuss today may be some of the most powerful stuff you're ever going to learn about business, and if you choose to take it on board, it may change your lives forever. But before we get started, what conclusions have you come to regarding what we've been doing over the last few weeks?"

"We've done great things with our product lineup, Coach. And we both agreed that our range is far too large. We've concentrated more on bread, and extended our range there by offering some exotic breads. We would, of course, drop most of our pastries because they're labour and time intensive, expensive, and of limited appeal."

The Coach was pleased to hear that Joe was really taking on board what he was saying. "That's great, team. That, along with the other strategies, should easily make your Delivery far easier and therefore, much better."

"We also think *Time Mastery* is the one area we're most in need of help, Coach," Joe went on. "We're both all ears on this end."

The Coach thought for a while, then said: "Time is your scarcest resource, and one you can never get more of. Before we begin to make changes or improvements here, you need to first do some good old testing and measuring. You need to have an idea of what you're spending your time on. I'm going to fax you over a table that I'd like you to complete. Live with this sheet for a week and make a note every time you do a specific task."

The fax machine purred into life and a sheet of paper printed out.

The Coach's Superquick Time Study

In order to grow your business, you'll need to carve 10 to 20 hours a week out of your busy schedule. Considering that you are probably working 60 to 80 hours, this may be difficult but shouldn't be impossible. Once you have some time to invest in team building and marketing, you'll see your business begin to grow. Let's find out where your time is going.

1 Fill in the chart below to estimate how much time you spend each per day of the typical week working in your business:

Day of the week	Hours
Monday	
Tuesday	
Wednesday	
Thursday	
Friday	
Saturday	
Sunday	
Total	0.0

2 Fill in the chart below with the 5 to 10 task categories you do on a weekly basis, e.g., communication (mail, phone, e-mail), delivery of products, bookkeeping, sales calls, meeting with clients, production time in plant, working front desk, etc.

Task	Hours
1	
2	
3	
4	
5	
6	
7	
8	
9	
10	
Total	0.0

Rework and refigure the numbers in these tables until the **Total Hours** in both tables are approximately equal. This will give you a good picture of what tasks are consuming most of your time. Now choose the one or two task categories that can be delegated. Your Coach will work with you to develop a plan to delegate one or two areas to other team members in your business or to a new recruit to your business. If you need to hire a team member, see our *4-Hour Format Hiring System.*

"That was fast, Coach," Nellie commented. She had always admired efficient people.

"Nellie, as you know, preparation is often the key to making the most use of your time. Now to your second piece of homework; for the next week I want you to keep a time log—that's a log of what you do every hour of the day in the business to see how accurate your estimates are on the time study I just sent you," the Coach continued. "Any questions on that one?"

"Do you want that at home and work, Coach, or just at work?" Joe laughed as he spoke.

"Yes, Joe, just at work. Now, getting back to this week's topic," the Coach said with a smile.

"There are two components to *Time Mastery*. They are *Goal Mastery* and *Self-Mastery*."

"First, let's work on *Goal Mastery*. Remember in our initial *Alignment Consultation* how we made sure you knew your goals and they were Aligned with your Personal and Business goals? Well that's where we'll start this lesson.

"Obviously the first key to *Goal Mastery* is having some. The second is putting them on paper as we did and, the third is to set what I call S.M.A.R.T. goals."

It was Joe who took the bait and responded.

"What are S.M.A.R.T. goals, Coach?"

"I'm glad you asked, Joe. They are goals that are *S*pecific, *M*easurable, *A*chievable, *R*esult-oriented, and have a definite *T*ime frame."

"That's very clever, Coach," he responded. "I like that."

"And it's easy to remember," said Nellie, eager to make a contribution.

"It's also very important to reward yourself or celebrate every time you achieve one of your goals," the Coach added.

Nellie picked up her pen and began writing as the Coach spoke his next few words.

Goal Mastery—
Having clarity about where I am going and where I am driving the business is vital to my success.

"What goals should we set first, Coach?"

"Well Joe, glad you asked," said the Coach as if he were waiting for them to ask.

"We need to cover a few of the basics of Goal Mastery that apply to every business."

"Start first by writing down your *Vision*. This is the overall 'goal' you want to achieve in business. It's like your guiding light or the overall purpose of your business. To put it simply, it should be truly inspiring and engaging for yourself, your team, and your customers."

"When I started my coaching business I decided I wanted to create 'World Abundance through Business Re-education,' or another example, one of my clients with a garden shop had the Vision of 'Creating the Best Garden Shop in the Country'."

"Wow, Coach, that's big dreams. Do you think it will ever happen?" Joe said what both he and Nellie were thinking.

"Joe, I'm not sure it will happen right away, but we are busy moving in that direction one business owner at a time."

"Great thinking, Coach," Joe was feeling a bit excited himself.

"Once you have that, write down your *Mission Statement*. The mission shows you and your team how you will reach your vision. It's about four major areas of your business; you'll see them on the fax I just sent through." Even the Coach was getting a bit passionate.

Vision and
Mission Statements

Vision—Your engaging and inspiring guiding light

Mission Statement—How you reach your Vision

What Business are you in?

Who is your team?

Who are your customers?

What makes you unique?

Culture Statements

Three Values that are important to you as the owner

Three values that are important to your team members

Three values that are important to your customers

Three values that are important to the success of the business

"Now, team, if you want examples of any of these you can see them on my Web site www.action-international.com and that way you can really start to understand what Goal Mastery for a business is all about," the Coach spoke knowing Joe and Nellie were still digesting his fax.

"Once you have your mission sorted out, you'll develop your *Culture Statement*. This lets you and, of course, those who join your team, know what's acceptable and what's not as they go about their job each day. Finally, you need to write down all the *Milestones* or goals that show you and your team that you're making progress towards the mission and vision of your business. If you remember, this is essentially what we did back at the time of your Alignment.

He paused momentarily to let what he had just said sink in. Then he continued.

"So, Joe, what then should your business Vision contain?" the Coach asked to check that they had understood.

"It's about where we want to go, Coach, and it needs to get me and my team passionate about what we're doing. It's almost like it has a meaning to it," Joe surprised even himself with how much he already understood.

"What, then, is a Mission Statement, Nellie?" Coach asked.

"The Mission Statement shows how the business is going to reach its Vision, Coach. It should state who you are, what business you are in, who your customers are, and what makes you different."

It was Nellie who now realized she'd learned a lot this session.

"May I just ask, what exactly is a Culture Statement, Coach?" Joe jumped in.

"In summary, Joe, it's your rules of the game. It's generally a 12-point statement that includes your three most important values as the leader of the business, your future and current team's three most important values, your customers' three most important values, and the three most important values to your company's success."

Joe was really getting his head around these goal-related concepts and he knew that Nellie would be enjoying them too. She liked this type of thing.

"I think that is enough for one week, folks. We'll talk again same time next week when the topic for discussion will be *Self-Mastery*. So until then, digest what you learned today and think about how you can use it. Oh, and work on your 90-day, 6-month and 1-year goals, your culture, your mission, and your vision."

"Sure will, Coach. That was fascinating. Talk to you again next week."

Nellie had prepared well for the next coaching session, and so had Joe. She had remembered what the Coach had said about the topic for the week and she had taken the note from the fax where the Coach had given them a head start on *Self-Mastery*.

Joe was looking forward to this session. He had always prided himself in his self-discipline; anyone who could start work at 3:00 a.m. each day and never take a day off other than for legitimate reasons would have to be self-disciplined.

Nellie, he knew, wasn't nearly as disciplined as he was. She had already admitted to him that she was looking forward to the session for precisely that reason. She was determined to improve in this area and would be paying particular attention.

"The first thing we'll cover today, folks, is the homework I gave you last week," the Coach said.

"Who's going to read it out?"

Nellie leaned closer to the speaker.

As Joe and Nellie went over their first attempt at their Vision, Mission, and Culture Statements, the Coach was very happy with their level of effort but still had to remind them that it usually took several weeks to get the wording right and make sure you were really showing the world your true goals.

Joe was excited about their Vision to be the Best Baker of Bread and Rolls in their town, and Nellie was truly passionate about having more clarity about their goals.

"As far as goals are concerned, Coach, I think we'll aim at pruning our product lineup within two months, to hire two additional employees by the end of the year and to increase our profit by 20 percent."

Self-Mastery—
I must use my internal discipline and the discipline of my Coach to keep myself focused and achieving.

"That's very good, Nellie, but what about your personal goals?"

"On that score, we aim to both be working a four-day week by the end of the year and to be spending more time with each other at home."

The Coach was impressed. He was impressed by their diligence as students, their passion for their business and for their coachability. They were truly moving forward and their business results were reflecting their newfound passion and knowledge.

"OK, now let's get on with taking a closer look at *Self-Mastery*. This is all about planning your day and then working your plan. Joe, you seem very well disciplined. What's your secret?" the Coach surprised Joe by getting him to lead the session.

"I've never thought about it, Coach, I just do what I have to do because otherwise no one else would do it. I guess I know what I want and I know what it will take to get there."

"Great thinking, Joe. It's really about being clear on where you want to go, what you have to do, and then working your plan to get there," Coach started directing them.

"So for the next few weeks I want you to e-mail me every afternoon a copy of what you are going to do the next day. Too often people wait until the mornings to plan their days. The best time to plan is the night before, as you're finishing your work day. That way you get to let your brain work on ways to do the job better overnight and you walk in with a plan in place. It allows you to be far more disciplined. Do you think you can do that each day, Nellie?" the Coach asked.

"Not only can I do it, Coach, but I think I'll enjoy it," was Nellie's reply.

"Great, can you lay your hands on the fax I sent you last week, the one that looks at how much time you spend at work?"

Nellie opened her file and pulled it out. Joe glanced over it and remembered the fun and frustration they had filling it in one night, when they realized just how far they had to go to achieve their goals.

The Coach's Superquick Time Study

In order to grow your business, you'll need to carve 10 to 20 hours a week out of your busy schedule. Considering that you are probably working 60 to 80 hours, this may be difficult, but shouldn't be impossible. Once you have some time to invest in team building and marketing, you'll see your business begin to grow. Let's find out where your time is going.

1 Fill in the chart below to estimate how much time you spend per each day of the typical week working in your business:

Day of the week	Hours
Monday	16
Tuesday	16
Wednesday	16
Thursday	16
Friday	16
Saturday	10
Sunday	10
Total	100

2 Fill in the chart below with the 5 to 10 tasks categories you do on a weekly basis, e.g., communication (mail, phone, e-mail), delivery of products, bookkeeping, sales calls, meeting with clients, production time in plant, working front desk, etc.

Task	Hours
1 Preparation	21
2 Baking	56
3 Cleaning	21
4 Maintenance	2
5	
6	
7	
8	
9	
10	
Total	100

Rework and refigure the numbers in these tables until the **Total Hours** in both tables are approximately equal. This will give you a good picture of what tasks are consuming most of your time. Now, choose the one or two task categories that can be delegated. Your Coach will work with you to develop a plan to delegate one or two areas to other team members in your business or to a new recruit to your business. If you need to hire a team member, see our *4-Hour Format Hiring System.*

She read out the numbers to the Coach, who made a note of them and then said: "OK, what we now need to consider is how you can free up around 20 hours a week, Joe, so that you'll have the time to work 'on' your bakery and not just 'in' it. A good place to start would be by delegating the cleaning duties. If you have no one you can get to take that over, think about hiring someone. Perhaps you could get a part-timer to do it for you."

Joe liked what he was hearing and knew that with their new growing profit levels, he could actually afford an employee to do this for him.

"Of course, you'll also have to cut down a lot further later on if you want to meet your goal of spending more time at home, Joe, but that can come later. For now at least you have identified where you can cut down so that you can spend more time working *on* your business."

Joe was beginning to feel more in control of his situation.

"Joe, I now want you to write a daily plan for your current position in the bakery. See, just by doing this you will most probably be able to prune a few extra hours off your heavy workload."

"You want me to do that now, Coach?"

"Yes, it won't take long. Start with Monday morning."

"OK. 3:00 a.m. open up; 3:10 fire up the ovens.; 3:15 begin preparing the dough and the baking pans."

"Stop there, Joe. I notice you spend 3 hours each day preparing things. Can you put a system in place to speed this up? I mean, can you write down the processes involved so that tasks that can serve two functions can be done together? Or, what about preparing enough dough to last the week? Would that be feasible?"

"Yes, for some products it would, Coach. That's a great idea. I reckon I could mix up enough dough to last the week for certain products on Sunday afternoon and then freeze it. We would need to buy a bulk freezer, of course."

"Good. Let's put that into the plan then. How long would it take?"

"I reckon only about 3 hours. Then that would cut down my preparation time each day from 3 hours to around 1 hour."

"Excellent, Joe. That means you have just 'found' yourself an extra 11 hours— 2 hours per day times 7 days less the additional 3 hours work on the Sunday to make the week's supply of dough."

Nellie was now beside herself with excitement, as she knew that was additional time they could spend together. She was a little hesitant about hiring people again, but knew the Coach was on her side and that she'd rely on his expertise to help them through.

The rest of the coaching call was spent tidying up the details of their new work plan.

Joe had suspected for a long time that, instead of owning his own bakery, all he actually owned was his own job. And it had come as something of a surprise when he and Nellie first started out in business that being your own boss wasn't all it was cracked up to be—for them.

At the time, he seemed to be working harder, longer hours and for far less than when he worked as an employee in the local bakery. While this was initially something of a letdown, he soon discovered after talking around that most small business owners were in the same boat. They were all working longer and harder than ever before, and many of them for even less than some of their employees.

Prior to meeting the Coach, he began to regard this as normal for a small business owner and he'd put many of his goals out of his head. Since he and Nellie had decided to become proactive and do something about improving their business by getting a Business Coach, his goals were suddenly looking like they might actually become a reality.

Nellie was particularly pleased they'd decided to take control of their situation, as she had been silently worrying about Joe. She never saw him much because he was always at work. Sure, she understood his reasoning, but she did worry that he would burn himself out, and where would that leave them?

She was so pleased that they were at last doing something positive with the bakery. And she was delighted to see that Joe was taking coaching seriously.

Coming to grips with the basics was a complete revelation for them because they really had no formal business training at all. Like the vast majority of small business owners, they were thrown in at the deep end. But at least they were not alone, so they didn't feel too bad about it. Like most others, they had only ever before reaped average returns at best.

At least now they were mastering their business on a basic level. They felt they were well on the way to having a real business, thanks to their Coach.

And this was what the Coach spoke about during his next coaching call.

"Getting rid of your job all those years ago is why you've got to understand the real definition of a business, Joe. My definition of a business is—a commercial, profitable enterprise that works without *you*."

"One more time so you can write it down..."

A business is a commercial, profitable enterprise that works without *you*.

He let that sink in for a moment, then said: "Make a note of that, and then make sure you display it in your office."

Nellie picked up a pencil and began writing.

Mastery is about the first part of the Coach's definition of a business— A *commercial*, profitable *enterprise* that works without me.

"You see, team, at *Mastery* you've got the first part done: a *Commercial Enterprise*. It's like building the foundations for a lot more to come.

"But Coach, that's nothing like what we've ever thought about," explained Nellie.

"I know my definition seems to be 180 degrees away from what you've been taught in the past, but think about it. The reason most people work so hard is because their business doesn't. Why build a job for yourself when you can build a true business, one that keeps on growing whether you're there or not?

"Is that possible?" blurted Joe.

"Remember this one simple fact. Your business is your product. It's what you're building, it's what you have to make work, and it's ultimately supposed to run without you," the Coach continued.

"That doesn't mean you have to leave, but it does mean you have to be able to have the choice as to whether you go to work or not. It's that choice and freedom that owning a business should deliver."

"Every business owner should ask herself a few simple questions. Am I too involved in my business? Can I pick up the phone in the morning and say to whoever answered: 'You all look after things, I'm taking three months off?' If you're like the vast majority of business owners, the answer would definitely be *no*. What does that show you? Do you have a business or a job?"

"*Wow*, Coach, way to make a point," Joe responded.

"It's for this very reason that you have to get yourself out of the day-to-day routine of the business, Joe. Stop working 3:00 a.m. till 7:00 p.m., doing the work *of* your business. It's like the carpenters that don't run their businesses. Instead they spend all day using a hammer and nails, working *in* their business.

"Imagine that when you started your business, you built it in your mind first, and then you drew a picture on paper of what it would be like when it was finished. That's right. You've got to finish a business at some stage and have it ready for sale."

"But Coach, I don't want to sell my business," Joe said.

"That's OK, Joe, but you still need to build it as if you might want to at some time. See, some people try to sell a business that hasn't been finished, so they're really only selling a *job*. Of course, they'd only ever get a fraction of the price for it."

"When you've got the finished picture, then you go to work creating that business. That means working *on* the business, rather than just *in* it. In fact, you're designing the business so it will run whether you're there or not. Then you've got choice, and as you've heard me say before, choice to me equates to freedom. You can keep the business or you can sell it. You can work in the business or you can spend your time more creatively elsewhere. That's what we will be discussing from here on in."

It had been three months since Joe and Nellie had taken on a Business Coach, and already they could see results. Not only had they physically done many things they didn't even know about before coaching began, but they also had an entirely different view about business in general.

Joe, in particular, had come to realize that the business was just a means to an end and not an end in itself. He now saw that he could one day run a successful business and have a life. He realized that the reason to have a business was to make having a successful life possible.

Nellie had also changed a lot since coaching began. While she always knew the importance of having a successful business, she now saw things with greater clarity. She had begun to focus more on the very reason they had the business, and this gave her a clearer purpose. She also realized that she couldn't succeed in business alone.

They were now very much more in control of both their money and their time. They understood, for the very first time, what they needed to do to Master the money side of the business, and they were loving it. They felt in control of themselves and their futures and it was a nice change.

They also knew exactly what they needed to do each month just to break even. This gave them the very minimum they had to do to remain viable—everything over and above this went towards meeting their monthly performance targets. It gave them something to aim for. They began to see it as something of a game and they liked games. Their business had become fun.

Nellie and Joe were taught that, in business, profit is king. And they understood the importance of concentrating on profit. They set a budget for profit: $10,000 a month. A budget for growth: 20 percent each year, and a budget for average dollar sale: $5.28, and they had started implementing strategies to get there.

Another aspect of running their business that had improved enormously over the past three months was that they knew their numbers, which allowed them to make sensible decisions for the future. They had mastered *Reporting*. They knew precisely what their *Average Dollar Sale* and *Margins* were. And they knew how to go about *Testing and Measuring*. They knew how to predict their future profit by measuring *Key Performance Indicators*.

Needless to say, much of what they had learned during the past three months was completely new to them. Like *Delivery Mastery*. They were surprised to learn that when it came to delivery, consistency is more important than brilliance. And they understood why.

The Coaching program had also produced some other less obvious, yet vital, results for Joe's Bakery, particularly regarding their use of time. Joe had been struggling with long work days for years, but didn't know quite what to do about it. In fact, he seriously didn't think there was anything he could do about it other than hiring another baker, and that had never worked for him.

The Coach got them to see that their productivity ultimately determines their success and profitability. He made them see time as their major challenge. They were able to put this into perspective through a time study, which highlighted areas where Joe could make changes. He did and was able to easily free up 21 hours of much-needed time each week.

Joe and Nellie also became a whole lot clearer on their goals, both business and personal, during the past three months. They also became much more disciplined and this helped keep them focused on achieving their goals.

Nellie had suggested they go out to dinner to celebrate the end of their first quarter under a Business Coach and Joe readily agreed. This was, he decided, to be part of their new lifestyle. He very much liked the idea of celebrating their successes.

As they entered the restaurant, they noticed their old friend Pete, who was just leaving.

"Hi, Pete," Joe said in surprise.

Pete too was surprised. He was also obviously pleased to see them.

"Well, how have things been going with you guys?" he asked.

"Great. Couldn't be better. In fact, we were saying only this morning that we have made so much progress since taking on a Coach that it's almost unbelievable."

Pete was genuinely pleased, and told his friends so.

"I'm really pleased for you. You know, so many people I come across wouldn't be as positive as you guys are. I mean, I would really hesitate recommending most of my acquaintances hire a Business Coach because I just know they would laugh at the idea."

Joe smiled and said: "Look who's laughing now. Boy am I glad I took your advice. We now know a whole lot more about managing our money and time. And it's paying dividends already. For one thing I work a whole lot less than I used to, and we're making more at the same time."

"Sounds like you've finished the *Mastery Level*, Joe," Pete continued. "Next you'll be concentrating on moving up to the *Niche Level*."

Joe began to look a little pensive.

"I don't know if we need to go there, Pete," he said after some thought. "I mean we are really happy where we are at now. We aren't the greedy type, if you understand what I mean. Perhaps we should just be grateful for what we have achieved so far and not push our luck any further."

Pete looked stunned.

"Are you crazy, Joe?"

He shot a quick glance at Nellie, who seemed equally stunned. Pete realized that this was the first she had heard about this.

"Look, Joe, I made the same mistake myself when I was where you are now. But the Coach convinced me to continue, and boy am I glad he did. See, the real benefits will only happen later, once you have gone through the entire program.

Believe me, hang in there, because what you still have to learn will blow you away. In fact, the Coach was showing me just the other day that he often works with clients who have already completed *Mastery* when he starts with them. He says that *Niche* is where the real benefits kick in."

Joe looked hesitant, and so did Nellie. But fortunately, she realized it would be up to her to reassure her husband and save a potentially embarrassing situation from developing.

"Sure we're going on with the program, Joe. Just think of the benefits we'll get. And besides, we really have no reason not to. It's not as if we can't cope or anything. It's not even that we can't afford it, because the coaching is paying for itself already."

She was looking squarely at Pete as she spoke because she was conscious of not wanting to put Joe on the spot.

"But let's discuss this inside, shall we? I'm starving and I'm sure Pete has other things to do tonight."

"Sorry to worry you, Pete, and of course you're right, Nellie. Our business is perfect for Niche Mastery and I do need to cut back my hours. Thanks for the words of encouragement, Pete. I owe you one."

"You'll do great, Joe; just give it your best shot," he said as he turned on his heel and was gone.

Part 2

▮ Niche

The dinner table was important in Joe and Nellie's household. It was there that much of their planning, discussing, and decision making took place. And it was there that they began putting things in place that would ultimately change their lives.

The latest flurry of activity was the result of a letter they received in the mail from their Business Coach. It contained background material about the next phase of their growth and development as business owners.

"Once I'm certain you have all the business fundamentals in place and therefore are no longer operating at the *Mastery Level*," the letter read, "I will concentrate on helping you *generate money* for your business. You will be at what I call the *Niche Level*."

Joe was puzzled.

"Coach, can you explain what a niche actually is? I mean I understand what the word means, but how does it relate to us and our business?" he asked Coach later that day.

There was a moments silence as the Coach gathered his thoughts.

"I suppose a niche could be thought as a position particularly well suited to the person or business who occupies it. And the beauty of this is that it means you control that market niche so you don't have to compete on price. You are accepted for the position you occupy and not the price you offer."

Joe grabbed a note from the Coach off of the fax machine.

Niche—

Once I am running smoothly at a base profit, it's time to find my market uniqueness and build my marketing and sales machines.

"I will remind you that at the Niche Level, the business will be viable and trying to make money. I will also constantly remind you that *niche equals no price competition.*"

"My main objective at this stage is to put sales and marketing strategies in place to create a niche for your business. I want you to realize that this will set the tone for everything we do from here on in."

"I will also be looking to identify areas where your business can be considered an *innovator*, because for a business to make money, it must exploit its own uniqueness."

Joe and Nellie were excited. They were now going to be moving into uncharted business territory and were eagerly looking forward to whatever challenges it would present.

"I first thing I want to do is re-introduce you to a very important business concept," the Coach began. "It's what I call the Business Chassis. Think of it as the backbone of your business. It is a powerful concept that revolves around the only five ways you grow your business. I'm going to fax it to you."

LEADS
(prospects or potential customers)

X

CONVERSION RATE
(the difference between those that could have bought and those that did)

=

CUSTOMERS
(the number of different customers you deal with)

X

NUMBER OF TRANSACTIONS
(the average number of times each customer bought from you that year)

X

AVERAGE DOLLAR SALE PRICE
(the average price of the items you sell)

=

TOTAL REVENUE
(the total turnover of the business)

X

MARGINS
(the percentage of each sale that's profit)

=

PROFIT
(something every business owner wants more of)

"Have you received it?" the Coach asked.

"Yes, we have it here," Nellie replied.

"OK, now you should also have the second page of the fax coming through," he said as the fax machine came to life once more.

The Five Ways—
The Business Chassis is vital to
growing my business, and if
worked well, it with help
me multiply my profits.

This was the call that Joe and Nellie found most interesting. They often said it contained the most powerful information they ever received. It was the call that the Coach said would be central to everything they would do from then on, and he was right. It changed the way they thought about business.

"Most people don't really understand business and, therefore, they work too hard," he began. "In fact, most business people work on the three areas of the chassis that refer to results, instead of the areas that can transform the business into a profit powerhouse. You'll see what I mean in a minute. First, let me explain the parts of the chassis."

Joe picked up his pencil and began taking notes. Nellie was way ahead of him and had been doing so from the beginning of the call.

"The first thing you need to remember is that it is vital to Test and Measure everything. So let's start with your *Number of Leads*. This is the total number of potential buyers that you contacted or that contacted you last year. Also known as prospects, or potentials. Most business people confuse responses, or the number of potential buyers, with results. Just because the phone is ringing doesn't mean you're seeing the cash. And, what's even more amazing is that very few businesses even know how many leads they get a week, let alone from each and every marketing campaign, each and every day."

"It's great to get a lot of leads, but then you've got to remember your *Conversion Rate*, which is the percentage of people who did buy as against those who could have bought. For example, if you had 10 people walk through your store today and you sold to only three of them, you'd have a conversion rate of 3 out of 10, or 30 percent. This has got to be a literal goldmine in almost every business I walk into. You've already got them interested; now you've just got to get them over the line. When I ask average business owners about their conversion rates, they take a stab in the dark and tell me it's between 60 and 70 percent. Just for fun, I get them to measure it, and a couple of weeks later we find out it's more like 20 or 30 percent. Imagine how you'd feel. You should feel great, in fact you should be excited, because if you're getting by at 20 or 30 percent, imagine how your business would run at 60 or 70 percent. Remember, double your conversion rate and you've just doubled your revenue."

Joe was intrigued.

"Is it usually as low as that, Coach? See, I would also have put our conversion rate up around the 90 percent mark, but from what you say, this is probably an area we also need to look closer at."

"You'd be surprised at what the actual number really is, Joe. Remember, you're in retail so yours should be higher than you'd see with someone in an insurance business, or a contractor like Pete," the Coach explained.

"That makes sense, Coach. Thanks," said Joe as he continued making notes while he spoke.

"Now getting to the next part of the Business Chassis: your *Number of Customers* is the number of different customers you deal with. You work it out by multiplying the total number of leads by the conversion rate. Remember, it's not about getting more customers—you can't change that number directly—it's about getting more leads and then improving your conversion rate. These are the variables that lead to your results.

"Your *Number of Transactions* is another of the five main variables of the Business Chassis. Some of your customers will buy from you weekly, others monthly, others on the odd occasion and others just once in their lifetime. What you want to know now is the average—not your best and not your worst, but the average number of times one of your customers buys from you in a year. Once again, here's another goldmine; most business people never collect a database of their past customers, let alone write to them, or call them and ask them to come back."

"That's a fantastic idea, Coach. I never thought of keeping a database of past customers," Nellie interjected. "I just assumed that once a customer, always a customer."

"Nellie, you'll be amazed at just how many ways we can ask a customer to buy from you again and again. So, next your *Average Dollar Sale* is one variable that at least some business owners do measure," the Coach continued. "Once again, some might spend $5000, some just $5, but the average is what you're after. Just a few dollars on each and every sale could be all it takes to boost your bottom line. Add up your total sales and divide it by the number of sales, just as you did when we worked this out last quarter. Remember, we've still got to grow this now."

Joe and Nellie were writing as fast as they could, trying to keep up with the Coach.

"Your *Revenue* is yet another result. Multiply the total number of customers you deal with, by the number of times they came back on average, and then by the average amount they spend with you each time. That's your revenue. Put simply, Customers x Transactions x Average Dollar Sale = Revenue. This is another area most business owners will know the answer to. Yet they most probably have no real idea how they got to it. Of course, you want more of it, but you can't get more revenue; what you can get are more transactions, a higher average dollar sale, and a higher number of customers you deal with."

"Coach, why isn't this taught in business school?" Joe joked along.

"I'm hoping one day it will be, my friend. Next it's your *Margin*—it's the percentage of each and every sale that's profit. In other words, if you sold something for $100 and $25 was profit, then you've got a 25 percent margin. Remember: this is after all costs have been taken out. It's potentially another little goldmine for you to tap into, probably even further than we have over the last 12 weeks."

"*Profits* are another result that every business owner wants more of, not realizing that they can't get more profit, but what they can get is greater margins on the revenue they've got.

"And that's it. The Business Chassis is the basic model that dictates the profit levels of every business on earth. By simply breaking down your business and marketing efforts (selling is married to marketing) into these five areas and understanding how each affects the other, you're halfway there—and way ahead of 90 percent of businesses out there."

Nellie finished taking notes and looked pleased with her efforts. She looked at them thoughtfully, then said: "Coach, is there a formula for the Business Chassis?"

"There certainly is, Nellie. It's on the fax I sent you."

Both Joe and Nellie read out aloud, as they scanned the Coach's note.

LEADS
(prospects or potential customers)

X

CONVERSION RATE
(the difference between those that could have bought and those that did)

=

CUSTOMERS
(the number of different customers you deal with)

X

NUMBER OF TRANSACTIONS
(the average number of times each customer bought from you that year)

X

AVERAGE DOLLAR SALE PRICE
(the average price of the items you sell)

=

TOTAL REVENUE
(the total turnover of the business)

X

MARGINS
(the percentage of each sale that's profit)

=

PROFIT
(something every business owner wants more of)

"Does that make sense team?" the Coach asked.

"Perfectly," Nellie replied.

"OK, let's look at an example. Let's assume we have a business that has the following figures:

Leads	**4,000**
	x
Conversion Rate	**25%**
	=
Customers	1,000
	x
No of Transactions	**2**
	x
Average $ Sale	**$100**
	=
Revenue	$200,000
	x
Margins	**25%**
	=
Profit	$50,000

Now, would you say that, with all the strategies I am going to teach you, it would be reasonable to increase all five of the variables by just 10 percent over the next 12 months?"

"Yes, I'm sure we can do that Coach," answered Nellie.

"OK then, let's do that, shall we? Here is what we will have:

Leads	**4,400**
	x
Conversion Rate	**27.5%**
	=
Customers	1,210
	x
No of Transactions	**2.2**
	x
Average $ Sale	**$110**
	=
Revenue	$292,820
	x
Margins	**27.5%**
	=
Profit	$80,525.50

"Can you see the effect a 10 percent increase in each area has had on the bottom line? It's resulted in a massive 61 percent increase in profits. But what would happen if we were to increase those variables by more than just 10 percent? Imagine the growth you could achieve. Just for fun and to show you how powerful this can be, let's rework the numbers with a 100 percent increase in each of the five, shall we?"

"Do you think that's possible, Coach?" Nellie asked with a bit of doubt.

"Anything's possible Nellie; it's not probable that we could do this, but as I said, it's just for fun.

Leads	**8,000**
	x
Conversion Rate	**50%**
	=
Customers	4,000
	x
No of Transactions	**4**
	x
Average $ Sale	**$200**
	=
Revenue	$3.2 million
	x
Margins	50%
	=
Profit	$1.6 million

"Isn't that truly amazing?"

"That's incredible, Coach," Joe said, almost unable to hide his excitement. "Even if we only get 10 or 20 percent in each area, we'll be doing so well."

"That's the thinking, Joe. Remember, the 100 percent is just for fun. Let's plug in your figures to see how your business shapes up, shall we?" the Coach continued, "Just fill them in; you should have them now because you've been collecting them after each coaching call, remember?"

Nellie flipped open her file and began talking and writing at the same time. "It's going to be so much better now, Coach, than it was 3 months ago, especially with the jump in our profit margins."

"Yes, team, 3 months ago with your almost nonexistent margins this would have looked ugly, and that, by the way is just one of the reasons we work on margins first," Coach replied.

Nellie went on with the numbers.

Leads (last month's total x 12)	**18,200**
	x
Conversion Rate (we sold to 2 in 3)	**68%**
	=
Customers	12,376
	x
Transactions (our best guess based on asking our customers and working backwards from the other numbers in the formula)	**11**
	x
Average $ Sale (on average back up again)	**$4.40**
	=
Revenue	$598,998.40
	x
Margins (on average)	**18%**
	=
Profit	$107,819

"Gee, Coach, that's really starting to look good," Joe said with some real pride.

"It feels good, team. When we work on the *Mastery Level*, we focus on your *Margins*. It's the most cost effective of the 'Five Ways to Grow your Profits.'" the Coach explained.

"Then, once the business owner has attained *Mastery* of the business, we concentrate on the next level, which is sales and marketing at the *Niche Level*."

"Here we start on the other four ways; *Average Dollar Sale* first, followed by *Conversion Rate*, then onto the *Number of Transactions* and finally we turn to your *Lead Generation.*"

"Why do you leave leads until last, Coach?" Nellie asked as she took more notes.

"It's generally the area that costs the most to work on. Advertising, for instance, is relatively expensive, especially when you're *Testing and Measuring* lots of different advertisements to find out which ones work and which don't. See, by the time we get to working on this area, enough extra money should be flowing into the business to cover the additional expenses."

The Coach had covered enough new ground for the week. It was time to hand out some homework.

"What I want you to do between now and our next coaching call is to refine your systems for *Testing and Measuring* your current average dollar sale, conversion rate, number of transactions, and leads to make sure we are starting with the right numbers."

"The emphasis is now on developing a niche for your business, and then implementing what I call your *Unique Selling Proposition* and *Guarantee* strategies," the Coach began.

"This is most important, as it underpins most of the marketing you'll be doing. So we're now going to discover your competitive advantage—your uniqueness—and then find ways to use it to develop a strong guarantee and position you in a *Niche* in the market."

"Great, Coach. I think I have something I'd call unique, if you know what I mean. But don't let me interrupt," Joe said with a grin.

The Coach didn't mind at all, and went on.

"What I'm talking about here is more than good service or a good price; it's all about knowing what makes you special, and being able to explain that to your customers in a way that shows them a benefit."

"Yes, I know what you mean," Nellie added. "You're talking about a point of difference, aren't you, Coach?"

"That's basically it. It's what I call your *Unique Selling Proposition*, or *USP* for short. It's the thing that sets you apart from your competitors."

Joe's Bakery's experience and situation was no different than that of thousands of other businesses. They struggled with the same constraints and challenges that just about every other business owner did.

"Once we've worked our way through this topic, and you've completed the questionnaires, you should know exactly what it is that makes you unique. But you might find that nothing makes you unique at all, and if that's the case, that's where the real fun begins. You see, we'll get to rethink your business by looking at it from outside the box, and we get to *invent* your new uniqueness."

Nellie was nodding to Joe. This was obviously something they had discussed in the past. She began writing as the Coach spoke.

USP and Guarantee—
My marketing needs to convey what
is unique about me and why someone
should buy from me today.

"You'll also have a full guarantee, written down exactly as it should be. This guarantee will be powerful. It will stop your potential customers dead in their tracks. The guarantee is heavily linked to your USP; in fact it can be the same thing. As a far out example, if you ran a funeral parlor that guarantees everyone will be smiling by the end of the funeral, you'd have a pretty attention-grabbing USP right there, wouldn't you? Once you've settled on a great guarantee, you might have to change the way you run the company, but it's vital. Here's a great example of a service-based guarantee: When you invest in a computer system with us, you get on-site placement, free consultation, and the security of 24-hour-a-day software and hardware support."

"I've even seen companies write a three-, four- or even a seven-point guarantee for their customers, removing the frustrations of dealing with their industry. Like the plumber who promised on-time service, to clean up after himself, and to only charge a callout fee if he could fix it today. That was a great three-point guarantee."

The Coach hung up after going through their questionnaire and explaining what he wanted them to do over the course of the coming week.

"This is going to be fun, Nellie," Joe said. "But it's an area where you're best to take the lead."

Most of the rest of the week consisted of throwing ideas around and modifying, discarding, or adapting USPs and Guarantees until they arrived at one they were happy with. Of course, they still had a way to go, but they were, at least, on track.

OLD-FASHIONED SERVICE WITH BAKING TO MATCH.

GUARANTEED TO GIVE YOU THAT "EAT SOME MORE" FEELING, OR YOUR MONEY BACK.

Joe was beginning to take to being coached. He found that he was not only learning more than he believed possible, but he was really enjoying himself as well. It had begun to enter his mind that "learning" about how to run a business properly was not above him; it was well within his grasp.

He actually found himself impatiently waiting for the next coaching session.

"From now on," the Coach began when he answered the phone a week later, "if you think of marketing strictly as an investment, of customers as something you 'buy,' then you'll start spending at least 50 percent of your time in this area of the business."

"I've seen today's session completely transform thousands of businesses who were stuck on the treadmill of traditional marketing thinking. Today is all about my rules of marketing. And we're going to go through a summary of each one."

Joe watched Nellie as she started taking notes.

Marketing Rules— Marketing is a process of following some very simple rules.

"I'll fax you a copy of my Rules in a moment, but be sure to listen and take notes," the Coach began.

"So many business people focus their whole lives on cost reduction instead of income growth. If you really want to make money, you've got to put more of your time into income generation than you do into cost cutting. Just a few hours a day focused on income generation can pay for the wages of several people.

"It's important to know that business has two major parts, and, both are equally as important. You've got to put 50 percent of your time, effort, and investment into distribution—getting your products and services ready and to the marketplace. The other half of your time should be invested on sales and marketing—getting the marketplace to come to your products and services. Generally the second half, getting them to come to you—is the one area that business owners know least about, and therefore, do the least of.

Joe knew the Coach was talking about him. He had only ever really baked bread and put it on the shelves; never had he or Nellie ever done any real marketing.

"If you're not focused on creating cash flow, then you're wasting your time in business. Think of marketing as an investment and not an expense. And test and measure everything you do, because if you don't, you won't know what's working and what's not. You'll really be gambling with your marketing funds, and to put it bluntly, marketing will be an expense in companies where you don't *Test and Measure.*"

"Instead of spending a fixed amount on marketing, when you take on the idea of investing in sales and marketing, you've got to understand that every investment has a purchase price. In business most people think that you just invest in the stock you sell—but the same is true of customers. As soon as you start to see your business as a total marketing entity, *not* a production, service, or retail entity, you'll understand why the price you pay for customers is generally your biggest investment."

"Sorry, Coach. You've lost me. Can you go into that with a little more detail for me?" quizzed Nellie.

"Sure thing, Nellie. You really do 'buy' your customers with your marketing.

Remember, that they come at a cost—a marketing cost. You have to run advertising campaigns, have brochures and specification sheets printed, provide demonstrations, offer guarantees, pay for a team of sales people, and much more. Finding those new customers is an expensive business. So to put this simply, if you run an advertisement for $1000 and you get 10 new customers, how much did you pay for each of them?"

Joe jumped in, "That's easy, Coach, $100 each. Now I get it."

"And Joe, we call that your *Acquisition Cost*." The Coach kept going, as he had a lot to get through today. "*Acquisition Cost* is important but, just chasing market share in today's business world is a guaranteed formula for chasing your tail. If buying customers is your biggest investment, then continually buying new customers, or *buying market share*, is the most expensive way to do business. Chasing *Wallet Share* is as simple as remembering that you've got a loyal customer base, so what else can you sell to them? You see, they already know you, they already like you—they've already bought from you—and they already know what you can and can't do for them. All you need to do is find a profitable way to ask them to buy from you again and again.

The Coach stopped for a breather before he kept explaining his marketing rules.

"Most business people define their business by what they sell. Like a fruit shop, an accounting service, and so on. Change from a product or service point-of-view to a marketing point-of-view and you'll realize you're now in the *profit*-making business. And, making a profit is as simple as spending less than you earn. In other words, you've got to buy customers, with your sales and marketing, for less than they spend with you, either by cutting the cost of buying a customer, or by extending the amount they spend with you over their lifetime of buying.

"To put this simply, you must establish a long-term view of the value of your customer before you can appreciate how important it is to develop a relationship with customers and to ensure everything is done to keep them for as long as you can. How much would a customer spend if she were your customer for life? How much would she send you in referral business and so on and so on? That's her *Lifetime Value* to you. Work out her *Lifetime Value* and your *Acquistion Cost*; bring your cost down and your lifetime value up."

Joe was stunned by what he had heard.

"I never knew this was marketing, Coach. I'm beginning to see it from a completely different point of view."

"It's time to get off the traditional 'creative' marketing treadmill and start getting somewhere in business, Joe," the Coach responded. "Think about it this way. If you buy customers for less than they spend with you, you can create an unlimited marketing budget. Let me give you an example. One of my clients, an accountant, ran advertisements that cost $600 and got 20 new clients each time, thus he invested $30 to buy each new client. Now, on average a client spent $480 on her first visit, so he spent $30 to buy a client immediately worth $480 in income."

"Coach, that's like turning money into more money, isn't it?" Joe interrupted.

"That's it, Joe, marketing is an investment when you *Test and Measure*," the Coach picked up where he left off.

"Once you've accepted these rules and are prepared to make the necessary changes to your business, that's when you can start applying the tips about each marketing strategy that we'll be working on over the next few weeks and months."

"Make sure you go through these rules and see what ideas you can come up with to apply them over the next week," the Coach said as they ended the call.

Nellie was putting the finishing touches to her notes as the Coach finished speaking. She slid the Coach's new fax over to Joe. He skimmed over the contents quickly and nodded.

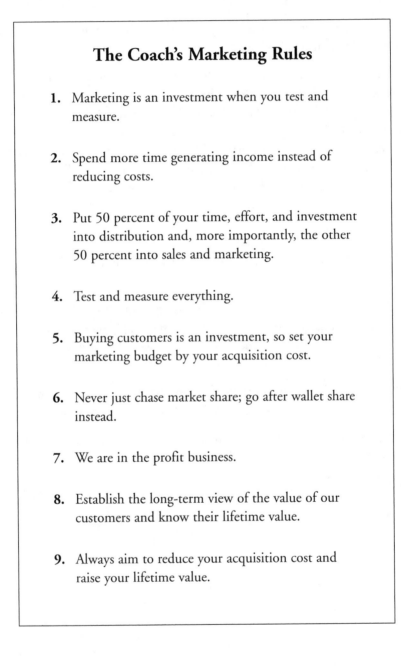

The Coach's Marketing Rules

1. Marketing is an investment when you test and measure.

2. Spend more time generating income instead of reducing costs.

3. Put 50 percent of your time, effort, and investment into distribution and, more importantly, the other 50 percent into sales and marketing.

4. Test and measure everything.

5. Buying customers is an investment, so set your marketing budget by your acquisition cost.

6. Never just chase market share; go after wallet share instead.

7. We are in the profit business.

8. Establish the long-term view of the value of our customers and know their lifetime value.

9. Always aim to reduce your acquisition cost and raise your lifetime value.

"The topic of this week's coaching call, folks, is less of a mystery to most business owners," the Coach began after he'd reviewed the team's homework at the start of the coaching call. "Yet precious little is usually done by them to increase it."

Joe was intrigued. He sensed that Nellie was too.

"I'm talking about Average Dollar Sale," the Coach explained. "Some customers might spend $500 while others spend only $23.50. The average dollar sale is just that: the *Average* Dollar spent from everyone who does business with you. It's easy to work it out. Just divide your total revenues by the number of transactions you've made.

"Just like McDonald's staff always ask if you would you like fries with that, you need to look for ways of increasing your average dollar sale. Even though most people say *no* to the fries, think of the millions of extra dollars McDonald's make around the world each day from those who say *yes*. Now think of a similar strategy that could unlock another goldmine for you.

"The key is remembering that it only takes slight improvements in each area to make a massive difference to your profits. These customers are already doing business with you, and any little extra you can add on is all cream."

Joe was pleased to see that Nellie was busy taking notes.

Average Dollar Sale Machine—
After margins this is the easiest and fastest way to grow my revenues and profits.

The Coach told Joe and Nellie that he wanted them to now think about what they could do to increase their *Average Dollar Sale*. He said they must then implement these strategies and test and measure the results over the next five weeks. He reminded them that they already knew their current average dollar sale number—$4.40—thanked them for their time and then hung up.

"OK, Joe, let's put our heads together, shall we?" Nellie said, eager not to lose too much momentum. "Let's come up with five strategies to increase our average dollar sale."

Joe nodded and waited for her to take the lead. This was clearly up her alley.

"How do we get people to spend more?" he asked. "I mean, what can we do other than simply asking them to spend more?"

"We could raise our prices, for a start. We haven't had a price increase in ages and it's long overdue," she responded.

"Nah, that would be like committing suicide. I think that's a dumb idea."

"Well, I don't. Let's include it in our list and we'll ask the Coach what he thinks, OK?"

Joe nodded, then said: "I think it would be better to ask our customers to buy something a little more expensive—you know, like getting them to buy a larger loaf instead of our standard size loaf."

"That's a great idea, Joe. And what do you think about offering them something in addition, like some rolls as well as a loaf?"

"I like it, Nellie; keep going."

She leaned back and stared at the ceiling.

"I reckon we could think about offering other products that customers could buy on impulse; you know, like sweets, chocolates, and perhaps magazines or newspapers."

Joe was becoming enthusiastic and began wracking his brains to come up with a suggestion that would impress his wife.

"What about offering a home delivery service for orders above a certain value?"

"I think that is a great idea, Joe. Well done. I'll certainly add that one to the list."

The very next morning they began implementing their chosen average dollar sale strategies and drew up forms for testing and measuring the results. Nellie reminded Joe that their Coach said this was crucial.

By the end of the fifth week of working with the Coach, they were pleased to discover that they had been able to increase their average dollar sale from $4.40 to $5.28. Some strategies had worked, others had not, but overall the results were great.

"I'm rather proud of our efforts, Joe," Nellie remarked. "That's a 20 percent increase—not bad in anyone's language."

It was time to report back to the Coach. He had already coached them through implementing the strategies each week and he wanted to hear how the results had come in.

Nellie picked up the phone and dialed the now familiar number.

"Hey, Coach," she said as he answered the call. "I have some good news and some bad. Which would you like to hear first?"

"Let's start with the not-so-good," he replied.

"OK. Our home delivery service didn't really produce the returns we were hoping for—so we dropped it after our test period of a month. We were very disappointed because we really thought that would be a winner."

"And what about the good news?" he asked.

"The good news is that the other four strategies worked amazingly well."

They could hear that the Coach was excited for them by the tone of his voice.

"That's fantastic, team. What's that done to your bottom line?"

"What do you mean, Coach?" Joe asked.

"Can you quickly redo your Five Ways Chart with your new Average Dollar Sale number in it?"

"Sure, give me a minute and I'll fax it through to you," Nellie replied as she picked up her pencil and began reworking the Business Chassis.

Leads	18,200
	x
Conversion Rate	68%
	=
Customers	12,376
	x
Transactions	11
	x
Average $ Sale (on average)	$5.28
	=
Revenue	$718,798.08
	x
Margins	18%
	=
Profit	$129,383.65

"What do you think, Coach?" she asked. "Our bottom line has increased by another $21,564."

"Well done, guys. That's a really great result. You should be proud of yourselves."

Nellie looked at Joe and they burst out laughing. Business had become fun.

The Coach then faxed through a short note to Joe and Nellie to prepare them for their next coaching session.

Conversion Rate Machine—
Getting more of the people
who already contact you to buy from
you is a very powerful way to grow
your customer base.

"This is where it all starts to really happen, Joe and Nellie," he said as he kicked off the session. "See, once you get people through your door you must make the most of every opportunity. You must turn those prospects into sales. You must also think about how you convert walk-by traffic into buyers."

Nellie knew what the Coach was talking about because this was the area she struggled with each and every day while Joe busied himself in back with the ovens.

"Conversion rates are often given little thought by the average business owner," he continued, "and invariably when I ask someone out of the blue what their conversion rate is, they take a wild guess. That's not good enough. You have to measure it."

Nellie could see the sense in that.

"Regularly, business owners greatly overestimate the percentages. I remember one who guessed he sold to 80 or 85 percent of people who called or came into his business. After some serious testing and measuring, we discovered the figure was nearer 18 percent. This came as a huge shock to the owner, but it also represents a tremendous opportunity."

Joe whistled in amazement.

"Think of the bottom line difference you can make by significantly boosting your conversion rate. If you can take your conversion rate from 20 percent to 40 percent, you've just doubled your revenue."

Later that evening, Joe and Nellie sat at the dinner table still buzzing with excitement and anticipation. They were eager to discuss how they were going to increase their Conversion Rate. Of course, the Coach had given them many things to think about on the rest of their call, but he really wanted them to come up with their own ideas.

"I think the first thing we could do, Joe, is to push the fact that we guarantee our products. That might take the uncertainty out of the decision for new customers, especially the wholesale ones. Together with this, we could collect some testimonials from our regulars, like Pete. We could offer all new customers one. What do you think?"

"I like the idea, Nellie, but I don't know if it will work. I mean have you ever come across a bakery that does this?"

"That's precisely why it may just work. And in any event, we should check with the Coach and test and measure to find out."

Joe was not convinced.

"I think we should be doing things like offering people a sample before they buy, especially passers by."

Nellie was impressed; although deep down they always knew things like this should be done, they had never had the discipline to get it into practice.

"Where do you come up with all these great ideas, Joe? I am impressed. And to think marketing isn't even your job!"

"It's just common sense."

Nellie nodded.

"Isn't that all good marketing really is, Joe?" she asked with a smile.

The next five weeks were fun. Nellie was spending just as much time testing and measuring as she was doing her "job," yet she had never had more job satisfaction before. It occurred to her that she was actually spending a lot of time working *on* the business instead of just *in* it.

As the weeks went by she began to get a clearer picture of the impact their new conversion strategies were having on their business. Each week the Coach guided them with their implementation and strategy ideas, making sure they stayed on track. Joe, who was more than anxious to see the result after the five-week test period had run its course, was hardly surprised to discover that their efforts had indeed borne fruit.

"Come on, Nellie, so what's the result?" he asked as she finished tallying the numbers.

"My figures show that our conversion rate is now 81 percent, Joe," she responded. "That's an impressive increase of 13 percent."

"And, you know what, I haven't measured it, but I'm sure we have more people coming into the store; we're converting more passers-by as well," Nellie was really starting to see the benefits of coaching, but also loved the certainty of measuring.

"Not only that, but we've been converting more wholesale customers as well with our new sales scripts. I can't wait to show the Coach," Nellie added.

It was with great excitement that Nellie dialed the Coach's number. She counted as the phone on the other end of the line rang and always marvelled at the Coach's ability to answer precisely on the third ring.

"Hi, Coach. It's Nellie. Just thought you'd like some feedback on our latest win!"

"Hi, Nellie. Yes, I sure would," the Coach replied.

"It's our conversion rate. You know all the ideas you've coached us on in the last few weeks? Well we've been able to increase it to 81 percent. That's an increase of 13 percent."

"That's fantastic, Nellie. Well done. Can you fax me an updated Five Ways Chart?"

"Sure Coach, I thought you would ask for one, so I have it ready now. Is your fax machine turned on?"

"It always is, Nellie. I'm standing beside it now."

"By the way, Coach, I haven't measured it, but I think we are getting more new customers by converting more passers-by," Nellie added.

"That's to be expected, Nellie. The synergy of the strategies is starting to kick in. For now it's okay that you haven't measured, but it's probably a good idea to start checking this. It's just as easy as going back to your daily number of customers and working it through. Great stuff, team," said the Coach, impressed with Nellie's diligence.

"By the way, team, I think it's time to hire yourself a couple of part-time helpers. Your work load is getting out of control," the Coach mentioned.

"Sure, Coach, anything in particular we should be doing?" Joe asked with a smile, thinking of all the work he could hand over.

The Coach briefly took them through how to hire a team member, promising to go into much more detail further into their coaching when it was truly needed.

Moments later the machine purred into life. Nellie hung up with a smile on her face. She took one more long, hard look at the piece of paper as she retrieved it from her fax before sliding open her filing cabinet and pulling out the manila folder that had the coaching label on it.

Leads	**18,200**
	x
Conversion Rate	**81%**
	=
Customers	14,742
	x
Transactions	**11**
	x
Average $ Sale	**$5.28**
	=
Revenue	$856,215.36
	x
Margins (on average)	**18%**
	=
Profit	$154,118.76

She felt really proud of their achievement. It meant, she knew, a further increase to their bottom line of $24,735.11 from just 5 weeks ago and a total of $46,299.76 from only 10 weeks ago.

"Once you've made a sale, you need to make another, and another, and another—to the same person," the Coach explained once Nellie had run through their latest successes with him. She looked over to Joe and nodded. They understood the importance of customer loyalty, as they had many who had been buying from them for years.

"You should know the statistics," The Coach continued. "They say it costs six to seven times more to get a new customer than it does to sell to an old one. It's no news flash, but it's true!

"Every single person who does business with you represents a gold mine of lifetime opportunity. You must collect their details, get to know them, treat them as special, keep in constant contact, and regularly invite them back as a member of the family. These people are either going to make you rich or make you poor."

Nellie began writing furiously.

Number of Transactions Machine— My existing customers are a massive asset that I should be investing in.

"But before we start looking at ways to make more money, do you know how many times your customers buy from you at present? We're talking averages here, not the best or worst case. If you don't have it up-to-date, then find out now. Remember, if you don't know what your average number of transactions are, how will you be able to gauge whether you've been able to increase it through the strategies you're about to put into place? And how will you know which of them are working and which aren't?"

Over the rest of the call, Joe and Nellie had been given plenty to think about. As soon as the coaching session was over, they began throwing around ways to increase the number of times their customers bought from them. They already knew what their average number of transactions was because they had been testing and measuring. Knowing this gave them hope because they were both convinced they would be able to get their average customer to buy from them more than just once a month.

"Any ideas, Nellie?" Joe began. He was always happy for her to take the lead in areas like this.

"I think the surest way of going about this is simply to provide a better level of service so that they feel special," she replied. "I know this sounds a little fuzzy, but I believe it is a great start."

Joe nodded but looked unconvinced.

"I think we should be doing more concrete things, like letting them know of the other things we sell, besides bread. Like special orders for birthdays and weddings."

"That's a great suggestion, Joe. And I guess the extension of that would be to simply extend our range—you know, we could begin selling other more expensive things."

"Yeah, that could be fun. What about having a product of the week? You know, we could feature a different nationality each week and really promote an understanding and liking for different breads. We could even create a bread lovers club."

"Hey, that's a brilliant idea, Joe. That could really work. Yes, I like it—I like it a lot."

Joe and Nellie were now so excited about their plans that they wasted no time in implementing them. They were now enthusiastically spending time working *on* their business and not just *in* it, and they were having more fun than they had had in a long while. Every day they made sure to track their results and make whatever adjustments they thought necessary.

The Coach pushed them and guided them every week and, before they knew it, five weeks had passed and they were able to sit down and objectively review their results.

"Just take a look at this!" Nellie said once she had completed adding up the figures. "Our average number of transactions has gone up from 11 to 16 a year already when I average it out over the next 12 months. That's an increase of 45 percent, Joe. How good is that?"

"That's incredible, Nellie. And do you know the best part? It was easy and it was fun, wasn't it? But isn't it time now to phone the Coach? He'll be really pleased to hear the results, won't he?"

Nellie picked up the phone and began dialing. This time she placed her up-to-date Five Ways Chart in the fax machine and waited for the faint sounds of electronic music that would tell her that the Coach's fax machine had answered the call.

She smiled as her copy began re-emerging from her phone/fax machine. The story it told warmed her heart.

Leads	**18,200**
	x
Conversion Rate	**81%**
	=
Customers	14,742
	x
Transactions	**17**
	x
Average $ Sale	**$5.28**
	=
Revenue	$1,323,241.92
	x
Margins	**18%**
	=
Profit	$238,183.55

Joe watched as she worked out the size of the bottom line increase.

"That's incredible, Nellie," he shouted as he read the numbers. "That's an increase of $84,064.79! It can't be."

"Work it out for yourself, Joe. It is true."

The Coach did warn them, though, that they would have to maintain their level of hard work to keep these numbers up along the way.

"This is definitely the most thought-about area of marketing, and obviously the most glamorous," the Coach began. The topic for the coaching session was *Lead Generation*.

"If you want to make a sale, you've first got to generate leads. And if you want to increase the amount of business you do, you need to increase the number of leads you generate. You need to get more people to visit or call your business with the view to buying from you."

No surprises here, Joe thought. But he knew there would be more to it than that, and he was right.

"How will you know you've been able to increase the number of leads you get, if you don't know how many you're getting right now?" the Coach asked. "I find it very interesting that when I ask most business people how many leads they get each week, they say they don't know. They simply have no idea what methods work for them and what don't.

"The first thing you need to do is to start measuring the number of leads you're getting. Start by asking people who come into your business, or phone, where they heard about you. And keep records.

"Remember, a few months back I told you to start doing this. I can't stress this enough. If there's one thing I show business owners when coaching them, it's this; if you don't know what's working and what's not, you can't possibly make informed decisions. And you'll never know which ads to run. You may keep running an ad that never results in a sale."

Nellie leaned closer to the speaker and asked: "Customers usually come from many different sources, Coach, and this makes it difficult to judge how each ad is working from sales results alone. It could be that we simply received more referrals that week."

"That's why you need to find out for sure," the Coach replied. "Update your tally sheet and include all the possible ways people could hear about you. These could include newspaper ads, television ads, radio ads, referrals, direct mail, flyers, Yellow Pages, or walk-bys. Then every time someone buys, ask the question; 'By the way, may I ask where you heard about us?' Nobody generally has a problem telling you. Make a mark on the tally sheet in the relevant column. Keep at it and ensure that everyone on your team does the same. Then, after two weeks or a month, tally up and get the figures."

Nellie completed her notes and thanked the Coach.

Lead Generation Machine—Once I have the machine running, it's time to put more people into the front end.

"You'll now have a far better idea of where your leads are coming from, Nellie. And you'll know exactly how many you are getting each day and week of the month. You might even be surprised at what this simple exercise tells you."

As the Coach went through all of the finer details around Lead Generation, Joe and Nellie were beginning to feel like this was going to be the most challenging area of marketing, and as they found out, they were right.

It had now become usual practice to discuss the coaching session at the dinner table. It allowed both Joe and Nellie to look at things objectively and at a distance.

"So what ideas do you have about how we could go about generating more leads, Joe?" Nellie asked as she pushed her plate aside.

"Considering that all we have ever done is to run ads in the local paper, I guess there's a whole lot we can do," he began. " Remember the ideas the Coach had. We could run our ad in the school newsletter as well. We could promote our specialties and ideas for school lunches. We could also distribute fliers in the area. And we could take this idea one step further by having our brochure included in the pharmacist's monthly invoice mailing. Other than those, I'm stuck thinking of anything else. Can you?"

Joe amazed Nellie. Usually he was full of ideas of his own.

"Maybe we could hold a competition or something that we could tie in with our school advertising."

Joe was more than pleased with what they had come up with as a start. After all, next week they would speak with the Coach again and get some more direction.

"Let's get started first thing in the morning, shall we?" he said.

Eight weeks later they were at the office analyzing the results of their testing and measuring campaign. It was a lot tougher than they thought at first, and they had relied heavily on the Coach's experience; he even had them reading books to increase their knowledge.

They were both grateful the Coach had been so patient with them over the extra weeks, as now they were starting to see the growth in their number of new customers.

"I'm absolutely staggered, Joe," Nellie said, as she leaned back in her chair and took a sip of her wine.

"Even though some of the strategies bombed, the ones that worked have worked great. I calculate we've had an 18 percent increase in the number of leads we get, Joe. That gives us an annual figure of 21,476 leads each year. And because we now convert 81 percent of those into customers, can you see what is happening to our business?"

Joe sat there speechless.

Time to get on the phone to the Coach, Joe thought as he picked up the new Five Ways Chart Nellie had just prepared. He didn't have to tell her; she already knew.

Leads	21,476
	x
Conversion Rate	81%
	=
Customers	17,395
	x
Transactions	17
	x
Average $ Sale	$5.28
	=
Revenue	$1,561,425.47
	x
Margins	18%
	=
Profit	$281,056.59

"Congratulations, guys, that's another almost $43,000 to the bottom line" the Coach boomed. "You've just broken the quarter-million-dollar profit barrier. I think this calls for a celebration. What are you doing on Sunday?"

Joe looked over to Nellie, hardly able to contain his excitement.

"What do you have in mind, Coach?" she asked.

"You'll be spending the day touring. See, I'm renting you a Porsche for the day!"

Joe and Nellie decided to celebrate the first seven months of coaching by going out to dinner after their day touring in the Porsche that the Coach had rented for them. They'd become used to celebrating milestones now and viewed this as a small piece of positive reward for their hard work.

Niche is about the second part of the Coach's definition of a business— A commercial, *profitable* enterprise that works without me.

"I can't wait to learn how to get it to work, and then to work without me," he said.

But this celebratory dinner was to be different than those they had enjoyed in the past. Nellie regarded it as something of a working dinner.

"Joe, I want us to review the past seven months tonight," she said. "I think we need to put things in perspective and to take stock, as it were. This will help us to clearly see the benefits we've had from having a Business Coach."

He nodded and placed their order. As they waited for it to be prepared, Nellie began outlining all the things they had done as a result of what the Coach had taught them about running a business. She talked about how they now tested and measured everything, how they better understood the need to work *on* the business instead of *in* it, and of all the new strategies they had put in place—and even a part-time baker and another part-time front counter person.

"We have had some awesome results, Joe. We have increased the number of leads, we have grown our conversion rate, we have seen our average number of transactions shoot through the roof, and we've pushed our average dollar sale up dramatically."

Joe felt justifiably proud.

"And look what this has done to our bottom line! It has blown it out of sight—beyond my wildest dreams."

Joe unfolded his napkin and began to write down all the benefits they had experienced.

Part 3

▌Leverage

Leverage—
Now that we have great
cashflows and profits,
it's time to put systems in place to
handle the extra work.

Joe picked up the note the Coach had sent them and began reading. He knew from what Nellie had said that he would find it interesting because this would benefit him most.

The name of the game at this level is efficiency. This is where we turn our attention to *systems*. You're working too hard now so we need to leverage your time. It's time to achieve more through your systems.

You see, as soon as the business is making good money, it's time to invest in systems that will run the company. But you need to understand that restraint is needed; it is imperative to get the systems in place first before growing the company by taking on too many new team members, even if the existing team—presuming you had one—is straining under the increasing workload.

Over the course of next several months we will be taking a closer look at the four types of Leverage;

❑ Structure Leverage

❑ How-To Leverage

❑ Management Leverage

❑ Technology Leverage

It was a few days until their next call, so Joe just put the note aside and made sure he kept his mind on the job. Still, he was worried about how hard Nellie was working; he made a mental note to talk to her about it at dinner that night.

"Coach, we have been doing some planning and one of the things we'd like to discuss with you this morning is whether you think the time is right for us to hire someone full-time to take over from Nellie at the front counter."

Joe was full of anticipation as he spoke. He was dead scared the Coach would pour cold water over their plan. They had talked about this at length and had already set their heart on it.

"What makes you want to go down this route, Joe?" the Coach asked.

"We feel Nellie could spend her time better doing other things like concentrating on marketing or customer relations, Coach. You know, she could leverage her time better."

"You obviously can afford to take on another full-time team member now that you've had some terrific wins as far as your profitability is concerned. How do you envisage finding the right person, Joe?"

"We thought we would run an ad in the paper and see who shows an interest, Coach."

"And how would you know whether those who reply will be what you are looking for?" "OK, it's time I told you about my recruiting system, the one that turns the tables so that you get people fighting to work for you."

"This I've got to hear," Nellie quipped.

"Start by writing a great ad that will get people to call in. Start by saying something like this: WANTED—PEOPLE WITH PASSION, or, If you're the superstar bakery assistant we're looking for, you'll be…

Then talk a little about the job; be specific about the type of person you're after, then ask those interested to call a certain number. On this number you will set up an answering machine with about a two- to three-minute message you record that tells them all about your company and the position they're looking to fill. Then you ask them to leave their details and answer three questions that you design for them. This process alone will result in many dropping out."

"Dropping out?" cried Joe. "We don't want any to drop out."

"Ah, so you have so much spare time that you can talk to the hundred or so applicants that are likely to respond?" the Coach replied. "If I were you, I'd prefer to spend my limited time doing something far more profitable."

"Mmmm," Joe responded.

"See, what I am showing you here is a deselection process, not a selection one," the Coach explained. "This way, we ensure that only those who are passionate enough about the job apply. What you do next is to go through the messages and as long as each applicant has the basic skills that the job requires, then they get invited to a group interview."

"A group interview?" Nellie interjected. "What's that?"

"It's when we get everyone in together and go through the history of the company, your stories, the future, and your Vision, Mission, and Culture. Then you ask them to get up and tell you why they are best suited to the job and a little of their background."

"Isn't that rather intimidating, Coach?" Joe asked.

"That's the whole point, Joe. See, many will feel it a little too uncomfortable and either won't turn up or they'll leave half way through. But let me explain a little about the process of the group interview to put this into perspective. The interview session is divided up into two sections. During the first you talk about your business and the position involved, then there is a short intermission during which the applicants are given time to think about three questions, namely what their best achievement has been to date, a little about their background, and what they can bring to the job. They are also told that they will, during the second half of the session, be presenting their answers in front all the other applicants and that if they don't think this is for them, they are more than welcome to leave. Here again, several will deselect themselves at this point."

Joe was intrigued.

"And this system works well, Coach?" he asked.

"It works brilliantly. You see, what this brings out is the 'heart' and 'soul' of those who have applied. You can always teach people new skills or ways of doing things, but the most important attributes of any team member is their passion and compatibility with the other members of your team. And that reminds me. Every member of your team will also be there to decide who it is that they want to work with. Everyone has a say."

Joe and Nellie were excited by what they were hearing and couldn't wait to begin the recruitment process.

"What I want you to do now is to begin planning your recruitment campaign," the Coach said, and after a short discussion of the finer details, the Coach gave them some encouragement and hung up.

Joe pushed the speaker button on his telephone as soon as he heard the Coach's voice on the other end of the line. It seemed just like yesterday when they had their last coaching call. How time flies when you are having fun, he thought.

After the Coach checked in with how Joe and Nellie were progressing with their search for a full-time replacement for Nellie, he got the team directed back onto the task at hand.

"Systems—this has to be one of the most misunderstood areas of business today, the Coach said as an introduction to the topic. "But it's the central theme to the next level of growth, Leverage."

"I find this rather strange because it's one area of business that's easy to implement, and one that will make your life, and those of your team members, so much easier. And it also happens to be something that will make your business run smoothly, efficiently, and profitably.

The fax machine kicked into life at Joe and Nellie's little office. It was another note from the Coach.

"As with most things in business, they can be simplified and made easy to implement. Here's a little note I like to make sure I remember what systems are for."

Save
Yourself
Stress,
Time,
Energy, and
Money.

Joe nodded in agreement but didn't say anything, as this was an area he knew little about. He also knew that Nellie would be, similarly, at a loss.

"I'm big on systems for another very important reason," the Coach continued, "and that's because they allow your business to *work*—instead of your working."

Joe coughed in anticipation.

"That's right. The reason most business owners work so hard is because their businesses don't work. There are no systems; everything is in their heads."

Joe liked what he was hearing; he knew this was something he needed to fix.

"Now take a moment and imagine a world class, great business, a business where the owner didn't have to work in it. Would that business still *work*? I mean would it function properly on a day-to-day basis? Would you expect that all the systems and people integrate to achieve the results you want and the results your customers want?"

Joe nodded his head.

"Of course it would. Let me say this again. Almost all business owners I've ever met work so hard for this one reason: their businesses don't work—they do. Everything about the businesses is in their heads, and they're the only ones who can do anything, so they're trapped."

Joe was taken aback and grateful the coaching session was taking place over the phone. Otherwise the Coach would have noticed his level of embarrassment.

"Most owners are like this because they don't trust anyone else to do the job. For some reason they believe that no one else can do the job as well as they can. They have to be in control."

Nellie shot a glance at Joe as if to say "I told you so."

"The problem is, without good systems, it's almost impossible to know that your employees will do a great job, or any job at all. All great leaders are good at delegating, so get used to the idea of systemizing and then off-loading some of your tasks! And by the way, once you've given your team members the job to do, let them do it. Don't jump in to save them; that way they'll never learn how to get the job done. All they'll learn is that you're the only one who can fix things, so you always will. Remember, sometimes you have to let them fall off the bike to learn how to stay on. Systems will help you do this."

Joe nodded slowly in agreement.

"I'm now going to fax you a short document; it's about the first stage of *Leverage*. Please read it and digest it."

As the Coach covered the rest of the details for the week, the fax machine hummed into life.

Structure Leverage—Getting the right people in the right places, with the right plan, moves my business away from people dependency to systems dependency.

"Okay Joe, now that we know your business is viable and profitable, we need to think about the various positions in your business, so we can ultimately ensure both you and Nellie aren't overworking yourselves and are in a position to leverage your time to the fullest."

There was a silence on the other end of the phone as the business Coach let them think about what he had just said.

"That's easy, Coach," Joe replied. "There's just me and Nellie."

"No, Joe, what I'm talking about is getting you to think of all the positions your business will have when you have finished building it, whenever that might be."

"But we are not building it, Coach. We did that years ago."

Again there was a silence.

"See, if you have no growth ambitions, that's fine, but you still need to think through the process. I mean, what if you needed to hire another baker in addition to the position you fill at present? Now would be the time to earmark that position, even though nobody might be filling it for the foreseeable future. You're also about to take on a second person at the front counter. And what about a bookkeeper, and so on?"

"The Coach is right, Joe. I think we need to plan for our future growth, and anyway we're both still working too many hours," Nellie added.

"So how do we go about it, Coach?" Joe asked.

There was a short pause.

"You start off by developing a chart of your business, or an organogram as it is called:

- Start with the head of the business, which is both of you as the owners. Put the name of your position down at the top of the chart and in the center. Draw a box around it. This is the top layer in your organization.

- Next write down the names of the positions that report to you. Now remember these positions are those that might one day be included in your business. Draw a box around each of them and connect them to your box by means of straight lines. This is the second layer in your organization.

- Write down the names of all the positions that report to the positions that occupy the second layer. Draw boxes around them and connect them with straight lines—known as reporting lines—to their respective second-layer positions.

- Carry on in this fashion until you have your entire organization mapped out.

"And there you have it—a detailed map of your business."

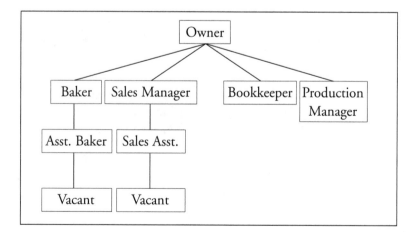

Nellie was proud of her handiwork. She wasn't much of an artist, but her ability to produce a neat-looking business diagram really pleased her.

"Okay, Coach, I guess the next thing you'll want me to do is to fill in names that go with each position."

"You read my mind, Nellie. But first, what about marketing? Are you going to have someone in there? And how about a Shop Manager? These are positions you might not have now, but will need as the company grows."

"You're right, Coach, we'll have to add those in," she shot a glance at Joe, smiled, and then began to pencil in names onto her diagram.

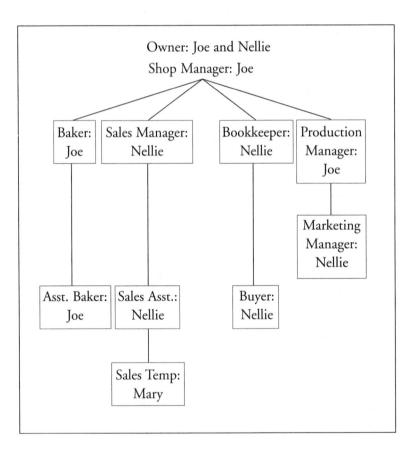

Joe was surprised at what he saw.

"Hey, Coach, when I look at this diagram, I can see why we are so tired. I'm doing four jobs and Nellie's doing six."

"And we haven't even talked about other jobs we know we need, but haven't got around to creating yet, Joe," Nellie chipped in. "If we were to get serious about this, and carried on the way we usually do, we'd end up doing even more ourselves and that's just not right."

"And you'd also run the risk of becoming a round peg in a square hole by being forced to take on tasks that you're not necessarily suited to," the Coach added. "By having a clear picture of what positions exist in your business, you can then decide on who is best to fill them. Of course, if there is nobody available, you can then begin searching outside your business for a suitable candidate."

Nellie picked up the piece of paper from the fax she knew was from the Coach.

Organization Chart Leverage— Getting the right people in the right places starts with knowing what the right places are.

Nellie had already read the Coach's fax and understood the need for *Position Contracts*. She knew it was one area of running a business that they were doing all right in. Even though the business consisted of just her and Joe, their areas of responsibility were clearly identified.

But she knew they would learn more about it during the coaching call, which was just about to begin.

"If people are clear on what they're supposed to be doing," the business Coach began, "they will do a better job. Every person is employed for a reason and has an important role to play. Let them know what that reason is and the part they play in helping the business to reach its goals."

So far so good.

"A person's *Position Contract* must clearly state the objectives, goals, responsibilities, and accountabilities of the position. It needs to state how the people doing the job will know when they have performed satisfactorily, when they have excelled, or when they have need to improve. It also needs to state tasks to be performed, standards to be met, and goals to be achieved."

Nellie made notes while listening to the Coach and passed the Coach's fax to Joe.

Position Contracts Leverage—
Giving people a clear picture
of their roles helps them achieve more.

"Coach, do we need to do this even for positions that don't yet exist?" Joe asked, and immediately wished he hadn't. He hated it when he asked questions before he even thought about the answer.

"Yes, you do need to Joe," the voice on the other end of the speaker replied. Joe started to relax as he realized there was no hint of malice or sarcasm in the reply.

"What we're going to do over the course of the next few weeks is to develop position descriptions for each role in your business, as well as position contracts for each employee. Remember, some people are doing more than one position, so you'll need to make their contracts a little different. Once this is all done, you'll then have a much clearer picture of your roles and what you need to do to achieve your goals. Any questions?"

It was now over to Joe and Nellie, and each week as they completed more and more of the task, they would have the Coach go through it with them and make sure they had things on track. It was reassuring to know they had someone like the Coach on their team.

Joe was looking forward to this session because he had always wondered what the connection between work and rewards was. The Coach seemed to have sensed his thoughts.

"Joe, there's no reason why you shouldn't be rewarding yourselves for achieving goals. But here's another thing you need to bear in mind. Your system of rewards needs to be fair and consistent, or it could backfire. It should be linked with *Key Performance Indicators* and be taken into account when considering promotions and salary or wage increases."

"What sorts of things are included in a typical *Key Performance Indicator*, Coach?" Nellie asked.

"They are normally the things you would use to judge whether a particular job is being done well, things that are central to that job. For instance, if you employ a sales person, you might measure her performance by the number of people she sells to each day, taking into account the number you set as a target. Or, if we're talking about you as a baker, we might measure the amount of waste you produce or the quality of your baking. This might be measured by customer feedback or returns."

"What things should we be measuring, Coach?" Nellie asked.

"You should be measuring *Key Performance Indicators* in all areas of the company—in fact, for each position, Nellie. You see, you cannot manage what you do not measure, so make sure everyone measures their *Key Performance Indicators*."

"So, overall for the company you have things like Leads, and Average Dollar Sale, all areas of the Five Ways. You might like to look at some others from your Balance Sheet and Profit and Loss as well."

"Then with each person you should set individual targets and link them to their bonuses. That gives individual team members something positive to strive for. It also adds an element of competition into their daily routines. By doing this, you ensure that people aim for, and achieve, their own individual goals. This will have positive effects on the running of your business and it will have positive effects on your team members."

Nellie began writing a note to remind herself of the main point before she forgot.

The Coach finished the call by going into more detail around financial ratios and other possible KPIs specifically for the Bakery. It was a leap for Joe and Nellie, but they knew if they were ever to run this business properly, they had to learn to understand new things.

Joe and Nellie had come a long way since they took on the Coach.

Key Performance Indicator Leverage— You cannot manage what you do not measure.

They knew their understanding of business was now light years ahead of where it was a few short months before, and by any standards they were doing all right back then. Of all their learning, it was the structure of a business that intrigued them most.

Getting the right people into the right positions, with the right plans, seemed to them to offer so many advantages because it would, they were convinced, move their business away from being so dependent on them in the future. It would relieve them of much of the burden that comes with being a business owner. They knew setting and measuring Key Performance Indicators would be crucial here. And it would mean they were really well along the path of creating an organization from their small business. Thank goodness through the first half of coaching they built on their income and profits to be able to afford to do all of this.

Joe and Nellie were now used to being coached and they understood what was expected of them. Joe had mentioned to Nellie just the other night that he didn't know how they had survived in business for as long as they had without a Coach.

How to Leverage was another area they were looking forward to discussing because it was one they thought they knew nothing at all about, probably because they hadn't had many other full-time people to worry about.

"Ever heard of the saying, 'people are a company's best asset'?" the Coach asked as a way of launching the new topic.

"I'm sure you have," he continued, not waiting for a reply.

"You have to give them every opportunity to do their jobs well and up to your expectations. Don't handicap them just because you never bothered to explain to them exactly how they should do their jobs and, for that matter, exactly what their jobs entail. And this is where systems really come into play."

"The best way to do this is by developing manuals, videos, audio tapes, or even a set of pictures to explain everything in detail. You've heard of 'how-to' manuals, haven't you?"

"Yes, Coach, those we're familiar with. I bought a set of 'how-to' books on woodworking not so long ago," Joe replied.

"Good, so you'll be familiar with the level of detail they go into. See, the reason I say you need to develop your own for each position in your business is because your people will eventually move on and leave you with a predicament—especially if they've been with you for a long while and become almost indispensable."

"So how will we go about writing these manuals, Coach?" Nellie asked. "We aren't writers and we've never done anything like this before."

"Writing each manual is like doing an audit of each position. Just write down exactly what it is that the employee needs to do from the time they arrive at work in the morning until they leave at night. And consider each day or month too, because there will be tasks that only need to be done infrequently."

"When you group together all the 'how-to' manuals, you'll have an instant Policies and Procedures Manual for your business. This is the key to developing a successful business because it will ensure that things run smoothly every time."

"Bear in mind that you could choose to photograph everything instead of writing about it. A friend of mine who runs a restaurant used photos to show how the kitchens were to look at all times. And it worked very well for him, so it might for you too. The main point to remember here is that if it is easier to ignore the system than to use it, you have a bad system."

"Make a note of this, will you?" the Coach continued. Nellie picked up her pen and began to write.

"How to" Leverage—
Now that people know *what* they have to do, it's vital to make it easy for them to learn *how* they should do it.

Bradley J. Sugars

The phone crackled into life again. "Remember that your position contracts show them what they need to do, and your How-To Manuals show them how to do it."

"I'm going to fax you something now to think about," Coach said as he fed a sheet through his fax machine.

Moments later a sheet of paper was in Joe's hand.

Routine versus
Exception Leverage—
Make a list of everything routine
and break it into time frames.
Always leave a way for someone
to handle the exception.

"So the first part of your homework this week is to come up with a complete list of every routine or repetitive task done in the business, each week, month, quarter or year. Make sense?" The Coach waited for a reply.

Both Joe and Nellie replied with a yes at the same time.

This whole discussion was raising questions in Joe's mind. He wondered how it would work, in practice, in an organization larger than what he had. And although he didn't doubt anything the Coach was saying, it was more a matter of his being able to come to grips with the concepts because he didn't have any experience working in a large business.

"Seems to me this can all get fairly complicated, Coach. I mean, how do the employees know how this applies to them? How do they know exactly what affects them and what doesn't?"

The Coach considered his reply. "You're right, Joe. You can make this extremely complex, but the reason for doing it is to make things simple, so let's aim to do this the simplest way possible."

They both agreed that would be wise.

The Coach continued, "It's linked to the organizational chart of your business. The next thing you need to do is to develop a flowchart for each area or department in your business: you know, in your case, the shop front, the administrative office, and the bakery. This chart will describe in detail what happens in each area. Think of it this way; it charts the path work takes through each department."

"That even sounds complicated, Coach. Where would we begin?" Nellie asked.

"Here's what you do," the Coach began. "Take one area at a time and work your way through it before tackling the next areas. You could start with the shop front, then move on to the bakery, and finally to the administrative office, because I would assume that's the path along which information would flow."

"That's probably about right," Nellie said.

"Start at the first point of contact with your customer. Document the flow of the job as it passes through that area, from start to finish, or until it passes through to the next area. Draw boxes around each function, like an incoming order from a customer, and then join them with straight lines. Bear in mind that incoming orders can be over the counter or via the phone, so that would be two separate functions. Get the idea?"

Nellie thought for a moment before replying.

"Yes, I think I do, Coach. I think it will be similar in look to the organogram. Am I right?"

"Yes, that's right, Nellie. Have a go with the shop front and see what you come up with. Remember that the reason is to show people how they, and the work they do, fit into your company."

She chewed on the end of her pencil for a while and then began to write.

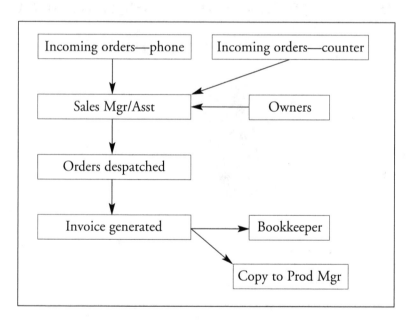

While she was doing that, Joe found himself grabbing another message off the fax machine from the Coach. This message would remind him of the main thrust of the coaching session.

Flowchart Leverage—
Everything has its place, and to
make systems work I need to show
people where it all fits.

Photograph, Document, Record, and
Checklist Leverage—
Now that I have a routine list that
fits together, I need to get to work
and write, record, or checklist
how it's done.

This was all the fax said when it came through. Joe knew who it was from and he also knew the reason for it: It was to be the main point of discussion during their next coaching session.

Joe was taking more than a slight interest in the topic of *Leverage*, because he could see that sooner or later they would have to think seriously about using these manuals in their business. He could see the benefits it would have for the business, as well as their lives, as they brought on more and more employees.

"Once you have a complete and detailed routine list of what your team members do on a daily, weekly, and monthly basis, your next task will be to document how they do it, or how they should do it," the Coach explained.

Joe nodded and instantly realized that his Coach, being on the other end of the phone, would not be able to see him.

"Uhmm, yes," he coughed.

"And we want to make sure we always look for the best way to do things. The Japanese have a great word for this. They call it Kaizen, and it basically means constant and never-ending improvement. Think of your quest for improvement as a circle. It has no beginning and no end. It's a never-ending quest. You just keep getting better all the time."

"How do we know if we're improving or not?" Nellie asked.

"Test each job one at a time. Start by comparing what is actually done with the KPIs. Are the KPIs being achieved? Are they all being achieved on time, or only some of them? What are the reasons for this? Can steps be put in place to correct this? Always look to make the systems better and easier to use."

"Once you've seen how each job scored, you need to involve your team members, and in your case it would just be the two of you. Get them to do the following:

- List their top 10 time-consuming tasks.

- List their top 10 stressful tasks.

- List their top 10 productivity-related tasks.

- List their top 10 tasks that bring them the most happiness.

"Now, how can they use the above four lists in their daily, weekly, or monthly routines? Can you streamline, adapt, amend, correct, or include something new here? Ask your team members to think about any bottlenecks they are aware of. Get them to list the three that they believe are causing the greatest problems to customers or your bottom line. You'd be surprised what your team members actually know about your operation—they do, after all, work closely with it day-in and day-out. Work at eliminating these problems one at a time. There will be a real sense of purpose and pride, and your customers should pick this up."

Joe was impressed.

"So that's how it's done! How would we go about writing the manuals?" he asked.

"It's not as daunting as you'd imagine," the Coach replied.

"Here are some considerations:

- Start with the work flow descriptions.

- Set out the chapter headings.

- Use bullet points and concise headings.

- Start with the first, or most important or regular task.

- Itemize each action that is needed to handle or complete each function, and write briefly what needs to be done.

- Mention what the desired outcome is, the KPI, and what happens next.

- Don't forget to mention what happens if things go wrong or another action is called for.

- And if possible use a videotape, audio, or even pictures."

"What I want you to do between now and our next coaching call is to write up the system for handling telephone orders."

"No worries, Coach. See you next week," Nellie replied and hung up.

Joe was on a roll. He wanted to get this done before he lost momentum.

"Okay, Nellie, what do you think? Let's get this done now, shall we?"

She nodded, opened her pad to a clean page, and began writing. Joe moved around so that he could see what she was doing. He spoke each word out aloud as she wrote.

When she had finished, she tore the sheet of paper from the pad and handed it to Joe.

"Can you think of anything else?"

He shook his head as he cast his eye over the document once more. Then he read it aloud once more in an attempt to come up with anything new.

"Handling Incoming Telephone Orders"

- When the telephone rings, the Sales Assistant will answer it after three rings.

- Say, "Good morning, thanks for calling Joe's Bakery; this is Nellie Speaking."

- When the caller says he wants to place an order, say, "Certainly; would you mind if I run through a couple of questions to ensure I get the details of what you want to order?"

- Reading from the sales script, which is written on the sales order form, obtain details of the order, the delivery address, and method of payment.

- Confirm the details with the customer by reading back the details to them.

- Thank the customer for the order and hang up.

- Make a copy of the completed order form.

- Send the original to the bakery and file the copy in the orders file.

- Write up a sales invoice, with two copies.

- Give one copy to the Bookkeeper, one to the Production Manager and put the original in an envelope ready for mailing."

They were excited that they had started. They knew they still had to run it by the Coach, but at least things were moving.

It was several weeks later that the How-To Manuals really started to fall into shape. Joe and Nellie had just employed their first full-time employee and felt as if a huge load had been lifted off their shoulders. Tamara had clearly been the one; she had shown real passion for the sales assistant job and had stood out head and shoulders above the seven others who turned up for the group interview.

Nellie had remarked that the group interview went far smoother than she had expected, and Joe agreed. In fact, he went further, saying that it was not only fun, but it gave him a boost of enthusiasm too.

Joe began thinking that the time was just about right for them to hire someone full-time to help him in the bakery. After all, he reasoned, the business was growing and they were finding themselves being required to work *on* the business and not *in* it more and more. They knew what a group interview involved and how successful it was. It would be, they knew, a simple process to run through again, because it was systematized.

Joe could see that as things were developing, his once simple bakery was rapidly beginning to resemble a much larger business, at least as far as structure and organization were concerned.

They were becoming involved in areas that were far removed from the hustle and bustle of the heart of any bakery—the place where the baking gets done. Yet this didn't worry them, as they could clearly understand the reasons why.

The more they discussed it, the more they began to question how all these systems would work together. What worried Joe was whether he wouldn't just be swapping one role for another once they began systematizing their business. The last thing he wanted was to end up behind a desk instead of in front of an oven.

He loved baking, and if he wanted a desk job he would have trained for one fresh out of school, instead of learning to be a baker.

He found himself beginning to resent this wave of change that was overcoming them. Strangely enough, Nellie didn't feel that way at all. She was the one who was positive about their outlook. And this was probably a good thing, he knew, because time after time she'd been the one who seemed to know best.

Joe called the Coach, just to get this off his chest, and after 5 minutes he made himself a note.

That evening at the dinner table, Joe slipped the short handwritten note to Nellie.

Management Leverage—
It's not enough to have a system for
how things get done. I need a system
to manage all of it.

"This just about sums up how I feel at the moment, Nellie. And I can sense you feel the same."

So it was with more than a little interest that he waited for the Coach to answer his questions on their next coaching call.

Bradley J. Sugars

Resource Management Leverage— Managing a resource is all about planning and budgeting.

Joe was keen to find out how this area of systemization could apply to a business as small as his, and as he'd already picked up the Coach's fax for the day, he asked.

"Team, we break down Management Leverage into the two main areas of a business, its physical resources and its people resources. Now the Resource side is relatively easy to understand, but the People one is where we have to make sure we know the difference between Management and Leadership. At this stage we're just working on the management, but we'll get to that in a moment. First up let's deal with Resource Management." The Coach was getting straight to the point today.

"Of course, you have to understand what your resources are. Give it a shot, team. What are some of your resources?" The Coach was prone to getting them to think for themselves.

Joe piped up, "The machine and oven time would be one area, and probably our stock would be another, Coach. Am I right?"

"That's right, and as business gets busier it's vital to plan everything from basic usage to maintenance, replacement over time, and any other items specific to making sure you have enough capacity to meet your demand."

The Coach continued, "And Nellie, what about stock? Do you need to improve your planning here?"

"I guess so, Coach, especially now that we're growing. We've been having to make special orders so we won't run out, and that's costing extra in delivery."

"Great, that gives you both something to focus on for the week." The Coaching calls were getting quicker and quicker as Joe and Nellie became more autonomous. The Coach did, however, invest another 25 minutes going over their questions and making sure they knew what had to be done.

People Management Leverage— Managing people is all about time and skill management, and then training.

It was at least 25 minutes into the next call before they even got to focus on what the Coach had for them this week, as most of the previous week's work needed changes and edits.

"Coach, do you think we need another week to finish the Resource Management work?" asked Joe impatiently.

"Probably Joe, but let's at least get you thinking about your People Management. So who can show me the difference between People Management and People Leadership?" the Coach said, knowing they still had a lot to get through on this call.

There was a short silence and Nellie was the first to speak. "Management is about having the right people and Leadership is about giving them direction, maybe."

"Great start, Nellie. Let's look at it in a bit more detail," the Coach said.

"In fact, let's examine a few of the basic things we can do to get this moving. First example is that you need to make sure you cover your bases by ensuring that, as far as possible, you and your team are cross-trained. I mean everyone gets sick, takes vacations, and has days away from the office for business or emergency reasons—and that applies to you too. Will this present a problem for your business if you were to come down with the flu? Who will attend to customers or the administration if Nellie or Tamara were to need time off work unexpectedly? And what would happen if you both decided you simply had to take a three-week vacation together? Will your new baker be able to shoulder the load alone?"

"A very good question, Coach, and one that has scared us silly, I can tell you," replied Joe. "We really are very lucky that we've never had to confront that question before now."

"Are you really lucky?" the Coach continued. "Just think about that for a moment."

As it became evident that there was to be no response to that question, the Coach pressed on.

"You need to develop contingency plans as part of your staffing system. Start with the Position Statements for each and every position in your business. Write down and clarify who does what whenever someone is away. This could follow lines of delegation or seniority within each functional area, or it could follow lines of reporting relationships.

The Coach went into a lot of detail around how they could cross train and manage their people well, and as he came to a close, Nellie pulled the phone closer.

"How about making sure we all know *how* to manage our time better, Coach?"

"That's an excellent suggestion, Nellie. People can double their output with only a little more input if they know how to manage their time. Time is a scarce resource and it's also nonrenewable. A little effort in time management can increase productivity enormously, which will have positive benefits for everyone in the organization. It means they can meet their own goals and company objectives easier. It helps them perform better, meet their Key Performance Indicators, and be in the running for a promotion or pay increases."

"So what do you suggest we do?" she asked.

"Consider attending a course on time management. It will not only upgrade your skills; it will also increase your morale and enthusiasm."

Joe and Nellie were now used to being coached and they understood what was expected of them. Joe had mentioned to Nellie just the other night that he didn't know how they had survived in business for as long as they had without a Coach.

People Management Leverage was really starting to get their interest now, probably because they now had other people to worry about.

"You've heard me say, 'people are a company's best asset'?" the Coach asked as a way of continuing the topic.

"It's true. People need to have their skills updated from time to time to remain 'relevant' to the business. Now I know this sounds a bit cold and impersonal and I don't mean it to, but the fact remains that people, like any other business tool, system or asset, need updating or they'll 'depreciate' and that's something we don't want."

"Looking after the well-being and welfare of your team members will not only make them feel relevant, wanted, and of value, but it will also help them feel competent and comfortable with their work. Content team members are productive team members, and this means a business that will function smoothly and profitably."

Joe muttered in agreement.

"What systems could you implement to achieve this?" the Coach asked.

"We could run an in-house training program," Nellie replied.

"That's right, Nellie. You see, you need to put things in place to ensure that you keep your people growing and moving forward, because that really is one of the best ways to ensure they keep the company growing. And when I say 'they' I include you two in that as well."

"What happens if our business isn't growing, Coach?" It was Joe who asked.

"I'm glad you asked this, Joe, because it is a business truism that if you aren't growing, you're dying, just like in nature. A tree either grows or dies; it can't stand still. There's no middle ground. The same is true for people in this information age. It's all about knowledge. Empower the people who work for you with appropriate knowledge. It will pay you handsome dividends."

"Won't we just be making them more attractive to the big bakeries in town?" Nellie asked.

"Don't worry about that. Sure, you might lose one or two, but think of the consequences if you don't train them—they might stay."

It took a second for them to realize that keeping an untrained person will cost even more and Joe finally looked to Nellie and they both nodded in agreement.

"So how do we train them, or ourselves for that matter?" Nellie asked. "What type of training should we receive?"

"Let's start with the first one. There are various types of training courses you could consider. These include:

- Induction training for new employees.

- On-the-job training where an experienced employee trains a newer employee.

- Departmental training sessions where groups receive formal training together.

- In-house training where the trainer is a team member.

- External training sessions or courses where team members are trained at external venues by external trainers.

- Specialist training where external trainers are hired to train team members in-house.

- Private training, where team members are encouraged to attend private training courses and are then reimbursed by the company on completion.

- Preretirement training where team members are assisted to prepare for retirement.

"The type of training you give depends on what type of business you run; let me read from my list as a guide for you."

- Technical training like baking bread, pastry, or cakes.

- Communication skills training.

- Supervisory skills training.

- Conflict resolution training.

- Computer skills training.

- Financial skills training.

- Management skills training.

- Telephone skills training.

- Sales skills training.

- First Aid training.

- Emergency training.

The Coach kept going and going until even he was ready to stop reading.

"The list is endless. But you do need to know what your options are so that you can build them into your 'How-To' system. Let's invest the next few weeks designing your Resource and People Management Systems.

As they finished the call, Joe and Nellie knew they were in for a few weeks of work, but they knew they were getting to a stage where it was really starting to become a business and not just a job for themselves.

Bradley J. Sugars

"So where do we start?" Joe asked. It had been several weeks since they started a new topic and Joe was just a little worried as technology was definitely not his thing.

"With simple things like scheduling and completing regular maintenance on all equipment," the Coach replied.

Technology Leverage—
Technology in itself is not the
solution, but using technology to
speed up our systems is a must.

"Have a good hard look at what systems you've created that technology can do better, faster, and more cost effectively. In fact, just think about the areas already using technology and think about how much easier it is."

The call went relatively quickly as Nellie really took hold of the subject.

"One major question though, Coach. How do we know that we can afford the new technology and that it won't go out-of-date the day we buy it?" Nellie asked.

"Nellie, I have a simple rule of thumb about investing in technology, and it comes in two parts."

"You see, some technology is at the front end of your business, like being the first to use a new technology that gives the customer a better, cheaper, more effective experience or product. I will always prefer to be at the leading edge here. However, always be certain to know that the market is truly moving, not just rumored to move. When it comes to background technology like a new software program for accounting, I'm less likely to hurry in. Either way. It's about the fact that you have to be able to afford it, or know that you have a way to afford it, before you buy."

"So you mean it has to work with our cashflow, Coach?" Joe was finally able to add something of value he thought.

"Exactly, Joe, especially for the bigger purchases. Remember it's the lease payments and long-term contracts that hurt companies most when they have a bad income month." The Coach was ready to end the call when Joe caught him by surprise.

"Coach, Nellie and I would like to take you to dinner some time soon, just as a way to say thanks."

The Coach had a slight smile as he replied, "That would be great, Joe. I'm glad to see your gratitude is still as strong as ever."

Leverage is the third part
of the Coach's definition of a
business—A commercial, profitable
enterprise *that works* without me.

Over dinner the Coach reminded Joe and Nellie of how far they had come.

At Mastery they had built a base level Commercial Enterprise, at Niche, they'd added the Profitable to their business. Now they'd completed Leverage and added the fact that their Business works.

Joe saw how far they still had to go, and was stunned when the Coach asked him where he was going to take his 2-week vacation in around 3 months.

"Coach, we can't possibly. We've got so much work and everything is just really starting to come together," Joe said as he tried to take another mouthful.

"Joe, Nellie, you're on track. Everything is moving toward the business running without you. It's time to start planning for a little more relaxation and only working the 20 or so hours a week you set in your goals," Coach was firm in his words.

After a few more worried looks and a few more words of encouragement from their Coach, both Joe and Nellie found themselves nodding.

It was agreed. They would vacation at the beach. It would be summer then.

Part 4

▎Team

In preparation for the next coaching call, the Coach had sent Joe and Nellie several pages of notes to read. It gave them a whole new perspective on team building and the confidence to take on additional assistance in the bakery. It also gave them a great note to pin up on the office wall.

Team—Now that we are profitable, have a great marketing machine, and can run systematically, it's time to build a solid team.

Joe had always thought of himself as just a small business owner or just the owner of a small business. He never really thought there could be anything other than that for him to aspire to.

It did surprise him when the Coach had said that, in reality, all he really had was a job, and a bad one at that. His boss was tough and he didn't get any overtime pay. The Coach said this was because he was doing all the work, taking all the risks, and originally, not even earning what he should as a business owner, both in terms of money and lifestyle. In all likelihood, back in the old days he would have been far better off working for a boss. Deep down inside, Joe had suspected this all along, yet before he worked with the Coach, he felt he didn't have any option but to continue doing things like he always had because he was far too deep into business now to change things.

And then he took on a Business Coach.

He had never before seriously considered the possibility that his bakery could ever work without his being there. He dialed the phone when it came time and began that week's coaching call with more anticipation than usual.

"Before considering ways to put together a 'dream team' in your business, it's important to consider just what a team really is," the Coach began.

"According to the dictionary, a team is a group of people who are on the same side. It's also a group organized to work together."

"Just like the players in a football team," Joe quipped.

"The overall feeling must be one of togetherness," the Coach continued. "Everyone in your company has a unique and equally important role to play.

None are more important than the others. You all have a distinct purpose in the overall well-being of your business."

Nellie thought for a while, then added: "So I guess it's important to build this into the structure of the business right at the beginning while it's still being built."

"Very perceptive of you, Nellie. And that's why you need to consider this now before you begin hiring many more people. But there's another dimension here that needs to be highlighted. Each team member not only has to fulfil her role within the organization, she also has to fit in with the rest of the team. You know the old saying that one rotten apple spoils the bunch? Well, it's true in business too. It all comes down to your company's culture. Finding the right culture match is vitally important when selecting team members. That's why I involve my whole team when looking for a new team member. You see, they're also the ones who have to live and work with the new team member, not just me."

"Here's another meaning of the word team: Together Everyone Achieves More," The Coach said. There was a silence, and then Joe remarked: "That's very clever, Coach, I can see the wisdom in it."

"And you know what?" the voice on the other end of the phone asked. "It starts with the owner of the business. My Dad always told me that I get the people I deserve. I didn't quite appreciate that at first, but now I understand what he meant. I now put it this way: life—and business—are just like a mirror; they're a reflection of you, meaning you only attract what you put out."

While he was speaking, the fax machine came on.

"Have a look at what I've just sent you, guys," the Coach said. "It will put what we are discussing into perspective."

Together Everyone *Achieves* More—
It's not about just feeling better; it's
about achieving more.

"You see, if you want a great team you have to be great leaders and run a great company. Average companies get average employees and so on," the Coach had really driven his point home.

Joe stepped in, "Coach, how do we know what a great company would look like and how to be great leaders?"

The Coach explained, "Team, that's your homework this week. Examine yourselves and your business. Would the best bakers in town want to work with you? And if not, what could you change to make it so they really want to join your team?"

After a little more explanation, Joe and Nellie knew it was the end of their time together today. It was time to get on with the job.

Joe was fully aware that everything goes around in cycles. He certainly knew that business was cyclical in nature, having experienced firsthand its ups and downs more regularly than he would have liked.

One of his longer-term goals had been to try to figure out a way to smooth out the ravaging effects this had on both his cashflow and the life of his family.

It had been several weeks of evaluating, changing, and making the company even better for their current and future employees when out of the blue the Coach called Joe and Nellie.

When the call came, the Coach started by explaining that the business cycle is a clearly defined process that involves four key players: the owner of the business, those who work in the business, the other businesses that supply the business with products and services, and the customers who buy from the business.

"Are any of these 'stakeholders' more important than the rest?" the Coach asked.

"What about the saying 'The Customer Is Always Right'?" Nellie responded. "Surely this implies that the customer is the most important of the four. I mean, without customers there would be no business."

"My view is that all four stakeholders are equally important," the Coach replied. "You see, without any one of them there would be no business."

"Good point, Coach," said Joe. "I have always had this sneaky suspicion that too much emphasis is given to the customer. I mean there are some I would rather not have."

"That's exactly my view. So let's take a quick look now at how each must be served by the business, shall we?"

"Go for it, Coach," Joe quipped.

"The business must serve the owners by providing them with profits. It must serve the team by providing them with recognition, rewards, and a paycheck. It must serve the suppliers by paying their bills. And it must serve the customers by fulfilling their needs."

Nellie was taking notes as the Coach spoke.

"Stand by for another fax."

Cycle of Business—The Owner supports the Team, the Team supports the Customer, the Customer supports the Business, and the Business supports the Owner, and around it goes again.

"That's so simple and straightforward, Coach."

"Most business concepts are, Nellie. What I want you to do now is draw a diagram of the Cycle of Business and think about how it applies to your bakery. Think you can do that?"

She said she could, and that brought the coaching session to a close. Then she started to draw. When she had finished, she slid the page across to Joe.

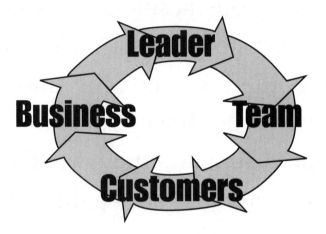

He looked at it for a while and when he had nodded in agreement, they began a far-ranging discussion on how it applied to their business.

Joe and Nellie had to call the Coach; they felt it was an emergency.

"Coach, what can we do? The new baker just quit on us this morning; we don't know what to do!" Nellie blurted before the Coach could even say hello.

"Calm down, team. This sort of thing happens all the time. Take a deep breath and let me run through it for you."

"When you hire new team members, you have the advantage of being able to impress upon them, right at the outset, what you expect of them, what the rules of the game are, and how they must go about performing their duties," the Coach explained.

"You see, they come into your organization fresh; they are totally unaware of any situation that might have existed previously, before you set about changing your company to meet your new objectives or goals."

"Experience with many businesses I've worked with shows that, when new systems or smarter ways of doing things are put in place, many existing team members leave. They become uncomfortable and don't like the idea of either having to learn new ways or having to move outside their comfort zones. So recruiting new team members becomes necessary. And this isn't always such a bad thing because these new team members will accept the situation they find as being normal. They are, therefore, usually very much easier to work with."

Joe had to ask, "So, this is normal, Coach?"

"Yes, Joe, not only normal, but healthy, and probably a good time to go into a little more detail about how we hire the best people," the Coach sensed they needed to be given something to do so they would be able to calm down.

Nellie was writing furiously as the Coach spoke. And then she noticed the Coach had sent her another fax.

Team Recruitment and Induction— Recruitment in great companies is about deselection, not just selection.

"A great team is one of the best assets a business owner or operator can invest in. The way organizations find or recruit team members is important, as excellent people can only enhance your business. Remember the group interview process? Now you will understand just why it works so well. But let's talk a little here about how you go about writing the ad to attract prospective applicants.

"Once you've decided what type of person you want to attract, how do you go about writing an ad that will make that person not only take notice, but actually want to call you?"

"You'd make the ad large with a catchy heading," Nellie responded. There was a short silence before the Coach continued.

"Most people wrongly believe that good ads have to be funny, well written, or visually dramatic. The truth is the very best ads work because of the strategy behind them. Here's a good analogy. If you've prepared a delicious meal and your dinner guests are hungry, they won't care what kind of plates you use. Put another way, if your message appeals to the people you're writing to, it doesn't really matter how you present it."

Nellie had seen the light, and smiled broadly to herself.

"Of course, there are things you can do to make your ad clearer, more direct, and more interesting, but these are definitely secondary concerns," the Coach went on.

"If your strategy is wrong, the best penmanship combined with the best graphic design in the world won't save you. The only things you really need to consider when writing copy for your ad are how to target it to the people you are trying to reach, what will make them respond, and what is the best way to communicate this to them through your copy."

It suddenly occurred to Nellie that she had often suspected most people got it wrong when writing ads. She also thought that the professionals also made it appear more difficult than it really was.

"These days some job advertisements result in an avalanche of replies, others just one or two. Either way you really need a system to cope when the phone starts ringing," the Coach continued.

"That's why running a deselection process, as we discussed earlier, is so beneficial, because you don't really want to spend all your time wading through all the applications, do you?"

"By the way, I prefer respondents to call in rather than to mail in their application like so many companies want them to do. This is because anyone can pay to have a great-looking resume produced, yet this will tell you absolutely nothing about the real person behind the application. You see, what you need to be concentrating on here is the 'hearts' and 'souls' of these applicants, not just their level of skill and past experience. This is generally not relevant as they're applying to work at a different company with a different culture, expectations, and ways of doing things. You want to find the best possible person for the job, not just any person who can do the work. You're ultimately looking for that one person who wants the job more than anything else in the whole world. You are looking for someone who is passionate about the job."

Joe was taking this all in, but also felt that his Coach was telling him the obvious. He realized that it was so obvious it flew in the face of conventional wisdom.

"When you have run your group interview, short listed the group, done your one-on-one interviews, and chosen your new team member, notify her of your choice as soon as possible to make sure she's still available. Then arrange a meeting, before she joins your team, to discuss salary details as well as various housekeeping matters like working hours, the dress code, and etiquette."

Nellie had a question eating away at her.

"What should we do about the other applicants, Coach?"

"Good question, Nellie. It's equally important to notify all the unsuccessful applicants, as they will want to know where they stand so they can continue with their job search. They may also have another job offer, in which case they'd want to be in a position to act quickly so as not to lose that one while waiting to hear from you first."

"How do you recommend we notify them?"

"You can notify them either by phone or letter."

Joe and Nellie were excited. They had forgotten their problems of earlier in the day and begun to see the potential that lay in their business and what it would take to unlock it.

Joe began thinking more and more about what he needed to do so he could spend more time working *on* the business instead of just *in* it. Nellie began thinking about what they would do with all the spare time they would have once they began taking on team members. They both knew that with their new marketing and everything, the business could now afford it.

Joe knew the key to their being able to achieve this goal lay in the quality of their team. They simply had to hire people they could rely on to run the bakery as well, if not better, than they had been doing it over the years.

They knew too that the Coach would throw some light on the topic when they next phoned in.

They were right.

"Selecting the right people is just the start to building a successful team for your business," he said as he began the weekly coaching session.

"It's just one of the many ingredients that contribute towards the making of a dream team. See, it's one thing to have great people working for you; it's another to have all the other important elements in place so that this team can become a winning one."

Joe's mind was racing as he tried to think ahead of the Coach.

"You simply can't expect your team alone to transform your business," the Coach continued. "There are other factors that come into play. Fortunately, these factors are controllable. It's up to you to ensure they are a part of your team."

Joe couldn't contain himself. "So, what are these factors?" he asked.

"I'll run through them one by one," the telephone voice replied. "Write this down first…"

Keys to a Winning Team—
Building a team that
achieves more is about
six key fundamentals:

1. Strong Leadership

2. Common Goals

3. Rules of the Game

4. Action Plan

5. Support Risk Taking

6. 100 Percent Involvement and Inclusion

"The first thing I want you to bear in mind is that when building a winning team, everything you do will be done against the backdrop of your culture, vision, and mission. These three elements will set the tone for the team. They get their enthusiasm and energy from this core, and they will judge all their efforts, achievements, and expectations against them."

The Coach paused, then said: "Can you see why it's vitally important we get this right up front?"

He took the silence he heard as confirmation.

"OK, here then are those six key fundamentals…"

1. Strong Leadership—I need to be a decisive and assertive leader so my team can have confidence in my direction.

"If your dream team isn't backed up and guided by strong leadership, the result will be like having a supertanker sailing the ocean without a rudder," the Coach explained.

"Strong leadership is crucial. Of course, by strong leader I don't mean an autocrat or a dictator. There may be instances where this type of leadership style is appropriate, such as in a takeover or merger between two companies, but generally speaking, a strong leader is something quite different. Understand that I'm not referring solely to the style of leadership here. I'm talking more about the quality of leadership."

"The hallmark of a strong leader is passion and responsibility. These two qualities really set them apart from ordinary or situational leaders. People always respond well to leaders who are passionate about their jobs, their businesses, or their lives. It's contagious; the entire team will find themselves motivated to perform at their very best when led by a passionate leader. "

"Of course, it's one thing to be passionate about what you're doing, but passion alone won't make you a strong leader. There's another quality that must go with it, and that's responsibility. You see, a strong leader is one who will also accept responsibility for the actions of the entire team. It's absolutely essential that the leader be able to make decisions in a decisive manner. It's the ability to follow through that counts—being able to see the consequences of managerial decisions through to the very end and to assume full responsibility for them."

This got Joe thinking.

"Coach, what is the difference then between a manager and a leader?"

"Managers tend to concentrate more on the technical side of business, directing people on the job, making sure tasks are done to set standards or expectations and ensuring that deadlines are met. This is why I call them technicians. You see, they are most concerned with those aspects that I class as body and mind. They concentrate on their team members' technical abilities and skills. However, as they develop and grow—as they become leaders—they will find their role has changed significantly. No longer will they be operating like a technician; they are delegating that responsibility to someone else. And this won't come easy. You see, you first have to learn to let go—to trust someone else. This 'grey area' or uncertain territory that they move into will certainly be outside their comfort zone. They will find themselves in an unhappy and worried mental state. This is what is known as perturbation. Think of it as an activity they'd view, initially at least, as an intrusion."

The Coach paused so that Nellie could complete her notes.

"The symptom of the shift from Manager to Leader is perturbation. The difference between a Manager and a Leader is really that the Leader takes a far greater interest in those areas I call heart and spirit."

There was a long pause as the Coach took a drink of water. Then he continued.

"A strong leader is one who fires on all 16 cylinders."

"Pardon?" It was Nellie's voice that interrupted.

"A strong Leader is much like one of the largest engines built, a powerful 16-cylinder engine: They must be firing on all 16 at all times."

"Why 16, Coach?" Joe asked.

"I'm glad you asked, Joe. They have 3 for the knowledge and 3 for the physical well-being. Now, most businesses only concentrate on these two areas. But there are two other areas that are actually far more important. Strong leaders must also have their 5 'heart" cylinders or their human side firing as well as their 5 cylinders that represent their 'soul' firing strongly. These heart and soul factors are more important than the mind and body factor, and that's why I say they are worth 5 cylinders each and not 3."

Joe was impressed.

"You know, Coach, that's always the way we have looked at it, but we thought we didn't really know too much about this stuff."

"Isn't that interesting? I have always found that most business owners know more about business than they give themselves credit for. Most should follow their instincts more than they allow themselves to. But there's another few things a strong leader needs to be, and that's decisive, inspiring, and a visionary."

"Isn't that a pretty big task, Coach?" Joe interjected.

"Think about it, Joe. Take yourself as an example. Think back 12 months. Think about your growth as a business leader for a moment. When you started out on our Coaching program, you were in reality nothing more than an overworked, glorified employee."

"Gee thanks, Coach, you know how to make a man feel good," Joe interjected.

The Coach went on, "Well, Joe, that's a sign of how far you've come. Now you are working more *on* the business than you ever did before and you're in the process of hiring your new team members. Your business has grown and so has its bottom line. Let's not forget that you really have grown enormously as a leader. You are taking some pretty big decisions about the future of your business and you haven't had any trouble doing that."

"Thanks, Coach. You're right. We've come a long way and sometimes we forget that," Nellie added.

2. Common Goals—I have to have a goal that not only everyone knows and believes in, but one where everyone wins.

"The next thing you need to do is to set a common goal," the Coach explained.

"You need to show every member of your team what the goal of your business is. You can't expect them to achieve results if they don't know in simple words what the overall goal that they must be aiming for is."

It was Nellie's turn now to ask a question.

"Where would we start, Coach?"

"Start with your Vision. Remember the Vision must be regarded as the central aim that engages and inspires the support of all your team members. It inspires them to do the things they have to do to meet their own individual goals.

"From the Vision, remember you developed your Mission Statement. Your goals are very much more specific activities that when achieved, help you on the way to your mission and vision."

Nellie was still a little puzzled.

"This is a little confusing. Could you explain, then, the purpose of goals, Coach?"

"Sure. By setting goals you give your business direction and focus, as well as movement and momentum. They are the shorter-term things that get the business moving. Everyone needs to have goals that collectively help the business progress in the direction of its ultimate vision. It's no use setting individual goals for team members that pull in opposite directions. You'll be surprised at how easy this is to do. For example, Joe might set his baker the goal of operating with no overtime, yet he might set his salespeople the goal of doubling the sales of bread, even though it is only possible to produce the additional loaves by operating shifts on overtime.

"So make sure you set *smart* goals. What are these? They are Specific, Measurable, Achievable, Results-oriented goals that have a Time frame. If your goals don't meet these basic criteria, they won't be of much use. You or your team won't be able to achieve them. They will be unrealistic and a waste of time."

"So, a Common Goal is a *must* for a high-performing team."

3. Rules of the Game—When I give my team a clear set of guiding rules, it's easier for them to get their job done.

"Next you need to set your rules of the game," the Coach explained.

"You must show your team what they can, and can't, do. You need to create the playing field. Everyone must know the rules. You must write them down and display them for everyone to see. Remember, if you don't give them the rules, you can't blame them when they go outside the boundaries."

"What type of things should the rules highlight, Coach?" Nellie asked.

"They detail what the standards and norms are. And remember, your rules will affect your culture, and vice versa. While on this subject, you must aim at establishing tight points of culture, or boundaries, across which your team members are not allowed to venture. Within these boundaries they can pretty much move about as they please. I call this a Loose/Tight Culture. Think of it like a game of basketball. As long as you obey the rules of the game, you can move about the playing field wherever you like. You are loosely controlled within the tightly bound playing field."

"That sounds like a sensible arrangement, Coach," Nellie remarked.

"It's a marvelous setup for any business to have, yet you'd be surprised at how many don't have any clear boundaries at all, Nellie. People learn the rules by trial and error and only find out they've broken a rule when someone else gets upset. This lack of boundaries forces them to have a multitude of work contracts to regulate each individual team member. You see, if they didn't, chaos would reign. But by having to rely on this tightly regulated setup within the playing field, most businesses sacrifice internal harmony, creativity, and team spirit. It's certainly a less than ideal situation that relies on policing instead of trust."

"I guess most people like to know where they stand in the work place, don't they?" Joe said.

"That's right, Joe. And remember, if you don't establish your company's culture or rules, your team will do it for you. You will end up with a *de facto* culture that most probably won't be to your liking or in the best interests of your company," added the Coach.

"You two are in luck; you've already written your culture statements, so you're well on track."

4. Action Plan—When I give my team a clear plan of who does what and by when, it's easy for them to commit and start working.

"Now, every business needs an Action Plan."

This brought an immediate question from Joe, who had developed something of an aversion to them over the years. It was probably due to the fact that he didn't understand them and thought of them as something accountants did, and he wasn't an accountant.

"Don't worry, Joe. You've already done this. You see, what we have done until now all contributes towards your Action Plan. You've already developed and given to your team their position descriptions. They know what their jobs entail and what their responsibilities are."

Nellie was, as usual, taking notes.

"Having positional contracts will also save you the agony of sorting out the involved and emotionally charged disputes that can arise through misunderstandings relating to what a person should or shouldn't be doing. This is particularly so when things go wrong in the workplace and fingers start being pointed."

Joe nodded to Nellie, who was still writing furiously.

"The second thing you need to do is to develop a strategy that lays down how results are to be achieved and why certain things are done.

"Thirdly, you need a tactic that spells out how results will be achieved. This will be your 90-Day Plan. It's actually a step-by-step plan of what needs to be done by when and who will be responsible for doing it. Once you've done that, you need to develop systems by which your team can achieve results, and tell them who is doing what by when. Once again, you've already done most of this."

5. Support Risk Taking—Some of my team will make mistakes because they're trying something new. Support them; it's the ones who make no mistakes that I often have to Coach even more.

"You must be willing to take risks. If you don't, your team will always lag behind and will not push the boundaries. Remember, your business is just like a tree; it's either growing or it's dying. There's no middle ground. It can't stand still," the Coach explained.

"That's all very well, Coach, but I don't think most people like taking risks," Nellie responded.

"You're absolutely right, Nellie, most people don't. They are risk-averse."

"Why is this?" she asked.

"It has a lot to do with their habits. You see, we do what we do because of well-ingrained habits. A habit is something we do automatically. But habits can be changed. It's been said that it only takes 21 days to instill a new habit—that's all. Just concentrate on doing something in a different manner for 21 days and it will become a habit. Or, concentrate on not doing something for 21 days and you'll lose the habit."

"But can everyone tolerate some level of risk, Coach?" she asked.

"Absolutely. The level varies from person to person, depending on the situation and the circumstances. This could involve their financial investments, gambling, or looking for a new job. In fact, many will tell you that life itself is a risk."

"Risk taking in business is slightly different in that it's usually tied up with the company's culture. If the owner doesn't encourage the team members to take calculated business risks, the business will progress conservatively towards its goals. It will most probably make slow, unspectacular progress. It will also most likely project a dull image. Its people will behave in an appropriate manner, not wanting to step out of line by pushing any boundaries. The company will most probably never develop anything unique and will shy away from operating at the leading edge. It will not be thought of as an innovator."

Joe was intrigued.

"Do some companies actually encourage their people to experiment with new ways of doing things?" he asked.

"Certainly. They reward their team members for innovation or improvements to the way they do things. Consequently, people who work for companies like this will feel invigorated, stimulated, and appreciated in the workplace. They will enjoy coming to work each day because they will have tremendous job satisfaction. Chances are too that they will always be willing to go the extra mile without having to be asked. They will willingly give their very best. They portray, through their actions and reactions, the face of a happy, vibrant company. This will be picked up by their customers, who will readily prefer doing business with them."

"Remember though, this isn't about risks for the sake of taking risks, it's about growing the company, and growth almost always requires trying new things."

"Everyone likes being associated with people who are moving forward, and it's no different in business. Kaizen, the Japanese concept of never-ending improvement, will be a living concept in the business, as the entire team will naturally be seeking to constantly improve the way they operate. Efficiency levels will go through the roof, with a corresponding noticeable increase in the bottom line. Success will become a self-fulfilling prophecy."

"Obviously, team, this is something we need to work on."

6. 100 Percent Involvement and Inclusion—Each member of my team is responsible for being involved, and as the leader it's my role to include those who are having trouble being a part of the team.

"The final point I want to make concerning putting together a winning team draws the previous ones together. And if these have been done properly, it should happen automatically."

Nellie began taking notes.

"It's all about having each and every member of your team giving your business *all* of their attention, effort, and commitment. You need to make sure everyone on the team is involved. And this involvement must be 100 percent by 100 percent of the team."

Nellie put down her pencil and leaned towards the phone.

"Isn't that the ultimate goal of every business owner, Coach?" she asked.

"Let me answer that by talking again about sports. Imagine a team took to the field and several members didn't really want to play. How much harder would the ones who wanted to play have to work to cover for the fact that some of their teammates were basically idly standing by?"

"That would be crazy, Coach, but I can see what you're saying. If some people don't do their job, the rest of us have to make up the workload or we all go backwards," was Joe's summation.

"That's for sure. And while we're on the topic of growing, let's make sure that you understand how important it is to have a team that is passionate, focused, and all heading for the same goal."

The Coach then set the team their homework of implementing everything they had learned that day, and it would be enough to keep them busy for a couple of weeks.

The Coach had worked with Joe and Nellie over the last few weeks to make sure their team building was going forward. They'd recruited several new team members and were training them in how to follow the systems. It was going well.

They all knew it was time to pull it all together, and about halfway through the coaching call, the Coach started on a new, but very familiar subject.

Communication—It's the oil that keeps the team machine moving, and you can never have too much of it.

"Another benefit of thorough communication is that your team will begin to see and appreciate the benefits of the systems you have in place to run your business. They will realize what's in it for them."

"So team, how can you make sure the team communicates the best they can?" the Coach asked. Of course he had many of his own answers ready, but being a great Coach, he knew that it was more important to ask good questions than it was to give good answers.

"Team meetings, Coach," Nellie jumped in.

"And, how about a team newsletter and memos, Coach," Joe wanted to add his part.

"Great team, so homework this week is to design your communication systems. Remember this. You can't communicate too much, but you can do too little team communication."

The Coach invested time going over some more of Joe and Nellie's questions, and finally they all got off the phone, knowing that this week's coaching homework was going to, again, keep them busy for a few weeks.

Originally, the more Joe got to know about being in business, the more he had begun to question why he had done it. As far as he had been able to ascertain, the negatives far outweighed the positives. He worked longer and harder than his friends who had jobs and he seemed to take home less as well. And on top of that he had all the worries of running a business.

As the years went by every now and then he would seriously weigh his options. He had yet to discover what all the fuss about being in business for yourself was all about.

Until he hired the Coach, that is.

"Why would you want to go into business for yourself?" the Coach asked of him at the start of the week's coaching call. "Just look at the statistics. It's said around 80 percent of businesses started this year will be gone in five years. Most business owners seem to work harder than any of their people, and many seem to make less income than they could make elsewhere."

Joe was glad they would be discussing this topic.

"So why do we do it then, Coach?"

"From what I've found, people start their own businesses for one thing and one thing only: *freedom*," he responded.

"Whether that is working for themselves, having more time to themselves, financial freedom, or just the freedom of knowing that they're in charge of their lives, freedom seems to be the main motivator."

"Isn't that interesting," Nellie said, not wanting to be left out of the conversation.

"Many people with little interest in ever 'captaining their own ship' argue that they're far from 'in charge' when exposed to the volatility of owning a business," the Coach continued.

"I retort with this analogy: I may have 100 different customers. You on the other hand have only one—your boss. If I lose half my customers, I still have 50 left. You just need to lose one to be singing for your supper!"

"That sums it up very well, Coach," Joe said.

"Yet despite this longing to be in charge, for most business owners, the exact opposite becomes the reality," the Coach went on. "Most end up having the business run them, instead of their running the business. In fact, they end up with the very thing they didn't want, a *job*." In effect, they've taken great risks and expended vast energy, and all they've done is bought themselves employment."

"I know exactly what you mean, Coach," Joe remarked. "I have pondered that very question long and hard myself over the years and have yet to find the answer."

"Well, perhaps your search will end today, Joe. See, getting rid of the *job* is why you've got to understand the real definition of a business: My definition—A business is a commercial, profitable enterprise, that works without *you*. I'll say that one more time. A business is a commercial, profitable enterprise that works without *you*."

Joe wrote as quickly as he could.

Team is about the third part of the Coach's definition of a business: A commercial, profitable enterprise that works *without me.*

The Coach paused for a moment to let that sink in.

"I know it seems to be 180 degrees away from what you've been taught in the past," the Coach continued. "But think about it; why build a job for yourself when you can build an income stream that keeps on growing whether you're there or not? Remember this one simple fact; the only reason you would ever start a business is to one day sell it. Your business is your product; it's what you're building for sale, and it's where you're ultimately going to make your profit— selling the business. Very few people ever make a fortune running their businesses, but a lot of people make a fortune selling them. Remember Bill Gates? He didn't become the richest man in the world by selling software packages."

"You make a very good point, Coach. But what if I don't want to sell it, Coach?"

"It's quite simple, Joe. Could you pick up the phone in the morning and say to whoever answered, 'You guys look after things, I'm taking three months off?' If you're like the vast majority of business owners out there, the answer would definitely be *no*. You might never sell it, Joe, but it has to be finished, it has to be ready for sale, and that means it runs without you."

After Nellie had replaced the receiver, she looked over to Joe and smiled. They had come a long way since they had taken on the Coach. They were both working fewer hours and their lives were without doubt less stressful. Nellie didn't have to shoulder the load at the counter any more; she had a team to do it for her. And what an enthusiastic team it was. Nellie felt comfortable entrusting them to run the show even on Saturday, their busiest day of the week. That meant she could enjoy her Saturdays at home with Joe, because he too was now able to stay at home thanks to Gavin, their new baker.

But perhaps the most surprising thing of all was that the bakery was now making more money than ever before.

Joe and Nellie really enjoyed their weekends together now.

Synergy was a new word for Joe and Nellie. When the Coach first mentioned it they had no idea what it meant.

"What is synergy, Coach?" Joe asked.

"It's something that is very important in business today. It's something that you must ensure your team has."

The Coach purposely avoided defining the word up front before he had a chance to emphasise its importance to the Joe and Nellie. He wanted to first tease out the concept a little.

"Synergy can be defined as the working together of two things to produce a result that is greater than the sum of the individual things. Put simply, it's like saying 1 + 1 = 4 or 5 or 6 or more. Think about it for a moment and you will realize that this is exactly how it works."

Nellie looked thoughtfully at Joe and nodded. She knew now exactly what the word meant and wanted to see if Joe did too. He nodded back.

"Synergy is a combination of individual 'things' that together produce an amazing result," the Coach went on.

"What goes into producing synergy will vary depending on your individual situation, but as you'll appreciate, it's not a complex phenomenon. In business, synergy is about building the four blocks we already have, *Mastery, Niche, Leverage,* and *Team* and following it up with the *Synergy level* of *Synergy Leadership.*

"It's about leading and growing the company; it's about watching from the outside to make sure all parts are working together to produce the desired outcome. You now have things working; let's do them bigger, more often, and faster than before."

"Can you give us a practical example, Coach?" Nellie asked.

"Sure. Take your marketing campaigns. Now that you know what works, when the plan is right, it's time to run more campaigns and build more income and manage the whole process. Or your budgeting and planning, what if you doubled the budgeted profit each month? What would your leadership need to do in order to make it all happen?"

Nellie was in her stride now.

"So synergy is just the end result of all our business-building strategies," she said.

"That's exactly right, Nellie. It's that magical something that occurs when all your systems and your team suddenly click together. It's what differentiates an ordinary business from a great business."

She looked down at the fax the Coach had just sent them and was surprised at what she saw.

Part 5

▮ Synergy

Synergy—
Now that everything is
coming together, it's time to turn
up the volume and make sure that
the outcome is far greater
than the inputs.

As the weeks went by, Joe noticed how everything started coming together and how his business had taken off. He marvelled at the power of synergy.

His keen sense of observation told him that his bakery was now in a very different position than what it had been before he took on a Business Coach. It also told him that in the last few weeks he had been busier than ever before and this, he knew, was not good. And even though the new team had found its feet and was performing well, there never seemed to be enough time in the day to do everything.

Nellie had pointed out that although the business was making terrific progress financially, in the last few weeks their lifestyle seemed to be suffering. And so too was the quality of their work, if they were honest enough to admit it.

Joe realized that cracks were starting to appear in their systems and this was beginning to have a detrimental effect on the business. He decided that he had to discuss this with his Coach.

"Hi, Joe," the Coach said when he recognized Joe's voice on the other end of the phone. "Just hang on a moment. I was wondering when you'd call, I have a fax for you. By the way, how are things?"

Joe grabbed the page from his fax machine as he chatted with the Coach.

Synergy Leadership—As we start to grow faster and faster, cracks will appear. I need to be a problem solver and keep one eye on the future with one eye on the present.

"Everything's going great, Coach, and I can't really complain. It's just that I'm beginning to feel like I am losing control. I have begun to notice cracks appearing here and there, and I am acting more like a fireman dashing about all over the place putting out fires, if you know what I mean."

"I know exactly what you mean, Joe, and it's quite normal. You see, you are growing, and growth brings with it its own problems. You have to act as the bakery's problem solver; there is no one else who can do that. You need to bear in mind that your team is still new and they're also having growing pains."

Joe was listening intently now. He wanted answers that would help him to stay on course and not throw in the towel.

"The one thing you need to avoid right now, Joe, is the temptation to either go back to square one or to grow the business too quickly by taking on more employees," the Coach continued.

"I know you'll be working a little more right now and feeling the load, but you must remind yourself that what you're doing is putting all the pieces in place so that your bakery will be able to function without you."

"What you'll be doing during this phase is building career planning into the business, carrying out cross training, appointing a manager, and fine-tuning systems so that you'll feel confident enough to finally let go of all the work. Synergy Leadership is about noticing the cracks that appear and either systematizing them or training your team to handle them. You can't see all the problems that come from growth before you grow, Joe."

Joe was nodding in agreement, "Uh-huh."

The Coach kept on going, "Once you are able to do this, you will be able to slide out of the business and still get incredible results at the same time. But to be able to do this, you need your team to be functioning really well in all areas of the business."

"Just knowing I'm on track means a lot, Coach. Thanks for the confidence boost," was Joe's parting comment.

Part 6

∎ Results

Joe's Bakery had come a long way since coaching began. Both Joe and Nellie knew that.

They had much to show for it, too. Not only had their financial situation improved dramatically, but so too had their lifestyle. They no longer felt tied to their business, and they felt in control of their future like never before.

The bakery was now a far more viable and secure business. It provided its owners with a reliable income stream, its team members with meaningful employment, and the local community with a good supply of affordable basic foodstuffs.

The regular coaching calls had become a feature of Joe and Nellie's lives and it was with a touch of sadness that they prepared for their final one.

"Hi, Guys, are you ready for your coaching call today?" the Coach asked.

"I think this is going to be a momentous one because it is officially the last one, isn't it?"

"That's right, Coach, it is," Joe responded.

"And for us it's a rather sad occasion, because they have become part of our lives."

There was a moment's silence before the Coach spoke.

"After a lot of soul searching and hard work, all the pieces are now in place for you to really enjoy the fruits of your endeavours. The bakery is forging ahead spectacularly from a business point of view, and it's time to reflect on just how far you have come through coaching. The final exercise I have for you, therefore, is to revisit the Business Chassis and rework the numbers by bringing them up-to-date. Can you do that for me now?"

"Sure, Coach," Nellie replied and switched on her computer.

Joe moved closer and watched as she opened up the page with their Five Ways Chart.

Methodically they plugged in the numbers.

Leads	**23,845**
	x
Conversion Rate	**83%**
	=
Customers	19,791
	x
Transactions	**19**
	x
Average $ Sale	**$6.21**
	=
Revenue	$2,335,140.00
	x
Margins	**23%**
	=
Profit	$537,082.20

Joe was still blown away by what he saw.

"What is it, Joe?" the Coach asked, hearing Joe's shouts of delight. "Still don't believe what you're seeing?"

"Coach, I knew we were doing OK, but this is madness! I mean it's over half a million bucks!"

Nellie was also speechless.

"Now I want you to take out your original Five Ways Chart that you completed a few months into the coaching and compare the two."

He had hardly finished speaking when Nellie hit the print button and spread the sheet on the desk in front of her and Joe. She read it out aloud quickly to remind themselves of the numbers.

Leads	18,200
	x
Conversion Rate	68%
	=
Customers	12,376
	x
Transactions	11
	x
Average $ Sale	$4.40
	=
Revenue	$598,998.40
	x
Margins	18%
	=
Profit	$107,819

She then turned on her calculator and began doing some calculations.

"Through the marketing strategies we put in place, we increased our number of leads by 31 percent, going from 350 a week to just over 458 a week. Then by paying more attention to providing great customer service, we increased our conversion rate from 68 percent to 83 percent. And that wasn't at all difficult. That gives us 19,791 customers, which is an increase of a staggering 60 percent. Our testing and measuring shows that our customers are now buying from us more often. Whereas in the past they bought from us on average about only once a month, they now come in and buy almost once every 2 weeks, or 19 times a year. And not only that, when they buy they now spend on average $6.21 and not $4.40 as they did previously. That is a whopping 41 percent increase. And once again, it wasn't at all difficult to achieve this increase. All we did was to ensure we didn't run out of product and we asked each customer if they wanted to buy something else while they were here. Our up-selling strategies worked beautifully. The net result of this was that our revenue shot up from $598,998.40 to $2,335,140. Of course, we don't get to keep all of this because we have to cover our overheads. So what do we get to keep? Wait, this is the best part. By managing the business properly, we have been able to increase our profit margin from 18 percent to 23 percent, which gives us a net profit of $537,082.20. If my math is correct, that's a huge 498 percent. This almost looks impossible, doesn't it, Coach?"

"No not at all, Nellie. It just goes to show the power of true leverage in business and what can be achieved by applying a few simple strategies to affect the different elements of the business chassis."

Nellie wrote hurriedly, not wanting to lose the thought while it was still fresh in her mind. This one she was going to have printed and stuck on her wall above her desk. It was a gem and she wanted to be sure to really take it to heart.

Results—Now that everything is running and growing smoothly, it's time to enjoy the fruits of our labor.

Joe and Nellie's lives had changed dramatically since they had hired themselves a Business Coach. Sure, their business hadn't become a bed of roses; it still had its challenges and it still had its ups and downs, but now they were in charge. They now ran the business, whereas previously it ran them.

Their bakery was now making good money—really good money. They were also able to lead well-balanced lives. Joe had taken up golf and was loving it. It had given him a healthy release valve and something he could get passionate about. Nellie was finally able to spend time each week enjoying the company of her friends. She really enjoyed their regular luncheons and visits to the theater.

Joe and Nellie knew their lifestyles were the envy of many and took delight in helping them to also reorder their busy schedules and regain some of the fun that they had been missing.

Nellie was proud of the fact that they had been able to put their business into perspective. As far as their lives were concerned, it had become a vehicle through which they could enjoy their newfound lifestyles.

They had become regular members of the local gym, and the benefits were just great. Not only were they able to tap into a new social circle, but their overall health and well-being took a turn for the better. They really felt good about life and about each other. They marvelled at the effects this had on their business as well.

Joe had become a different man. And he knew it all started when they hired a Coach. He also knew that they would never again go it alone in business without a Coach.

Joe had one comment for anyone thinking of hiring a Coach, "You've just got to do it."

▌ Review of Key Terms

MASTERY

The first stage of growing any business is about making sure we deliver profitably, productively, and with enough information to make great decisions.

Money Mastery

Not only do I need to know my historic numbers, but also the ones that will create my future.

Break-Even Mastery

Know how many sales, customers, or dollars I need to make per day to break even. And then how many to hit my profit goals.

Profit Margin Mastery

I can set a budget for profit each day, week, or month and implement strategies to get there.

Reporting Mastery

It's vital to know my numbers each day, week, and month so I can make decisions for the future.

Test and Measure Mastery

I can predict my future profits by measuring the KPIs in my business.

Delivery Mastery

Consistency is more important than brilliance. Stop any leaks, as there is no use filling the tub if the plug is left out.

Time Mastery

My productivity and the productivity of my people will determine my success and profitability.

Goal Mastery

Having clarity about where I am going and where I am driving the business is vital to our success.

Self-Mastery

I must use my internal discipline and the discipline of my coach to keep myself focused and achieving.

Mastery

Mastery is about the first part of the Coach's definition of a business: A *commercial,* profitable *enterprise* that works without me.

NICHE

Once I am running smoothly at the base profit, it's time to find my uniqueness and build my marketing and sales machine.

Five Ways

The business Chassis is vital to growing my business, and if worked well, it helps me multiply my profits

USP and Guarantee

My marketing needs to convey what is unique about me and why someone should buy from me today.

Marketing Rules

Marketing is a process of following some very simple rules

Acquisition Costs

Lifetime Value

Test and measure

Average $ Sale Machine

After margins this is the easiest and fastest way to grow my revenues and profits.

Conversion Rate Machine

Getting more of the people who already contact you to buy from you is a very powerful way to grow your customer base.

Number of Transactions Machine

My existing customers are a massive asset that I should be investing in.

Lead Generation Machine

Once I have the machine running, it's time to put more people into the front end.

Niche is about the second part of the Coach's definition of a business: A commercial, *profitable* enterprise that works without me.

LEVERAGE

Now that we have great cashflows and profits, it's time to put systems in place to handle the extra work.

Structure Leverage

Getting the right people in the right places, with the right plan, moves my business away from people dependency to systems dependency.

Organizational Chart Leverage

Getting the right people in the right places starts with knowing what the right places are.

Position Contracts Leverage

Giving people a clear picture of their role helps them achieve more.

KPI Leverage

You cannot manage what you do not measure.

"How To" Leverage

Now that people know *what* they have to do, it's vital to make it easy for them to learn *how* they should do it.

Routine versus Exception Leverage

Make a list of everything routine and break it into timeframes.

Flowchart Leverage

Everything has its place, and to make systems work I need to show people where it all fits.

Photograph, Document, Record, and Checklist Leverage

Now that I have a routine list that fits together, I need to get to work and write, record or checklist how it's done.

Management Leverage

It's not enough to have a system for how things get done, I need a system to manage all of it.

Resource Management Leverage

Managing a resource is all about planning and budgeting.

People Management Leverage

Managing people is all about time and skill management with training

Technology Leverage

Technology in itself is not the solution, but using technology to speed up our system is a must.

Leverage is about the third part of the Coach's definition of a business: A commercial, profitable enterprise *that works* without me.

TEAM

Now that we are profitable, have a great marketing machine, and can run systematically, it's time to build a solid team.

T.E.A.M.

It's not about just feeling better; it's about achieving more.

Cycle of Business

The Owner supports the Team, the Team supports the Customers, the Customers support the Business, and the Business supports the Owner—and around it goes again.

Team Recruitment and Induction

Recruitment in great companies is about deselection, not just selection.

Keys to a Winning Team

Building a team that achieves more is about the six key fundamentals.

> **Strong Leadership**
>
> **Common Goals**
>
> **Rules of the Game**
>
> **Action Plan**
>
> **Support Risk Taking**
>
> **100 Percent Involvement and Inclusion**

Communication

It's the oil that keeps the team machine moving, and you can never have too much of it.

Team is about the fourth part of the Coach's definition of a business: A commercial, profitable enterprise that works *without me*.

SYNERGY

Now that everything is coming together, it's time to turn up the volume and make sure that the outcome is far greater than the inputs.

Synergy Leadership

As we start to grow faster and faster, cracks will appear. I need to be a problem solver and keep one eye on the future with one eye on the present.

RESULT

Now that everything is running and growing smoothly, it's time to enjoy the fruits of our labor.

Getting into *Action*

So, when is the best time to start?

Now—right now—so let me give you a step-by-step method to get yourself onto the same success path of many of my clients and the clients of my team at *Action International.*

Start testing and measuring now.

You'll want to ask your customers and prospects how they found out about you and your business. This will give you an idea of what's been working and what hasn't. You also want to concentrate on the five areas of the business chassis. Remember:

1. Number of Leads from each campaign.
2. Conversion Rate from each and every campaign.
3. Number of Transactions on average per year per customer.
4. Average Dollar Sale from each campaign.
5. Your Margins on each product or service.

The Number of Leads is easy; just take a measure for four weeks, average it out, and multiply by 50 working weeks of the year. Of course you'd ask each lead where they came from so you've got enough information to make advertising decisions.

The Conversion Rate is a little trickier, not because it's hard to measure, but because we want to know a few more details. You want to know what level of conversion you have from each and every type of marketing strategy you use. Remember that some customers won't buy right away, so keep accurate records on each and every lead.

To find the Number of Transactions you'll need to go through your records. Hopefully you can find the transaction history of at least 50 of your past customers and then average out their yearly purchases.

The Average Dollar Sale is as simple as it sounds. The total dollars sold divided by the number of sales. The best information you can collect is the average from each marketing campaign you run, so that you know where the real profit is coming from.

And, of course, your margins. An Average Margin is good to know and measure, but to know the margins on everything you sell is the most powerful knowledge you can collect.

If you're having any challenges with your testing and measuring, be sure to contact your nearest *Action International* Business Coach. She'll be able to help you through and show you the specialized documents to use.

If, by chance, you're thinking of racing ahead before you test and measure, remember this. It's impossible to improve a score when you don't know what the score is.

So you've got your starting point. You know exactly what's going on in your business right now. In fact, you know more about not only what's happening right now, but also the factors that are going to create what will happen tomorrow.

The next step in your business growth is simple.

Let's decide what you want out of the business—in other words, your goals. Here are the main points I want you to plan for.

How many hours do you want to work each week? How much money do you want to take out of the business each month? And, most importantly, when do you want to finish the business?

By "finish" the business, I mean when it will be systematized enough so it can run without your having to be there. Remember this about business; a little bit of planning goes a long way, but to make a plan you have to have a destination.

Once again, if you're having difficulty, talk to an *Action International* Business Coach. He'll know exactly how to help you find what it is you really want out of both your business and your life.

Now the real work begins.

Remember, our goal is to get a 10 percent increase in each area over the next 12 months. Choose well, but I want to warn you of one thing, one thing I can literally guarantee.

Eight out of 10 marketing campaigns you run *will not work*.

That's why when you choose to run, say, an advertising campaign in your local newspaper, you've got to run at least 10 different ads. When you select a direct mail campaign, you should send out at least 10 different letters to test, and so on.

Make sure you get at least five strategies under each heading and plan to run at least one, preferably two, at least each month for the next 12 months.

Don't work on just one of the five areas at a time; mix it up a little so you get the synergy of all five areas working together.

Now, this is the most important advice I can give you:

Learn how to make each and every strategy work. Don't just think you know what to do; go through my hints and tips, read more books, listen to as many tapes as you can, watch all the videos you can find, talk to the experts, and make sure you get the most advantage you can before you invest a whole lot of money.

The next 12 months are going to be a matter of doing the numbers, running the campaigns, testing headlines, testing offers, testing prices, and, of course, measuring the results.

By the end of it you should have at least five new strategies in each of the five areas working together to produce a great result.

Once again I want to stress that this will work and this will make your business grow as long as *you* work it.

Is it simple? *Yes.*

Is it easy? *No.*

You'll have to work hard. If you can get the guidance of someone who's been there before you, then get it.

Whatever you do, start it now, start it today, and most importantly, make the most of every day. Your past does not equal your future; you decide your future right here and right now.

Getting into *Action*

Be who you want to be, *do* what you need to do, in order to *have* what you want to have.

Positive *thought* without positive *Action* leaves you with positively *nothing.* I called my company *Action International,* not Theory International, or Yeah, I read that book International, but *Action International.*

So take the first step—and get into *Action.*

■ ABOUT THE AUTHOR

Bradley J. Sugars

Brad Sugars is a world-renowned Australian entrepreneur, author, and business coach who has helped more than a million clients around the world find business and personal success.

He's a trained accountant, but as he puts it, most of his experience comes from owning his own companies. Brad's been in business for himself since age 15 in some way or another, although his father would argue he started at 7 when he was caught selling his Christmas presents to his brothers. He's owned and operated more than two dozen companies, from pizza to ladies fashion, from real estate to insurance and many more.

His main company, *Action International*, started from humble beginnings in the back bedroom of a suburban home in 1993 when Brad started teaching business owners how to grow their sales and marketing results. Now *Action* has nearly 1000 franchises in 19 countries and is ranked in the top 100 franchises in the world.

Brad Sugars has spoken on stage with the likes of Tom Hopkins, Brian Tracy, John Maxwell, Robert Kiyosaki, and Allen Pease, written books with people like Anthony Robbins, Jim Rohn, and Mark Victor Hansen, appeared on countless TV and radio programs and in literally hundreds of print articles around the globe. He's been voted as one of the Most Admired Entrepreneurs by the readers of *E-Spy* magazine—next to the likes of Rupert Murdoch, Henry Ford, Richard Branson, and Anita Roddick.

Today, *Action International* has coaches across the globe and is ranked as one of the Top 25 Fastest Growing Franchises on the planet as well as the #1 Business Consulting Franchise. The success of *Action International* is simply attributed to the fact that they apply the strategies their coaches use with business owners.

Brad is a proud father and husband, the chairman of a major childrens' charity and in his own words, "a very average golfer."

Check out Brad's Web site www.bradsugars.com and read the literally hundreds of testimonials from those who've gone before you.

■ RECOMMENDED READING LIST

ACTION INTERNATIONAL BOOK LIST

"The only difference between *you* now and *you* in 5 years' time will be the people you meet and the books you read." Charlie Tremendous Jones

"And, the only difference between *your* income now and *your* income in 5 years' time will be the people you meet, the books you read, the tapes you listen to, and then how *you* apply it all." Brad Sugars

- *The E-Myth Revisited* by Michael E. Gerber
- *My Life in Advertising & Scientific Advertising* by Claude Hopkins
- *Tested Advertising Methods* by John Caples
- *Building the Happiness Centered Business* by Dr. Paddi Lund
- *Write Language* by Paul Dunn & Alan Pease
- *7 Habits of Highly Effective People* by Steven Covey
- *First Things First* by Steven Covey
- *Awaken the Giant Within* by Anthony Robbins
- *Unlimited Power* by Anthony Robbins
- *22 Immutable Laws of Marketing* by Al Ries & Jack Trout
- *21 Ways to Build a Referral Based Business* by Brad Sugars
- *21 Ways to Increase Your Advertising Response* by Mark Tier
- *The One Minute Salesperson* by Spencer Johnson & Larry Wilson
- *The One Minute Manager* by Spencer Johnson & Kenneth Blanchard
- *The Great Sales Book* by Jack Collis
- *Way of the Peaceful Warrior* by Dan Millman
- *How to Build a Championship Team*—Six Audio tapes by Blair Singer
- Brad Sugars "Introduction to Sales & Marketing" 3-hour Video
- Leverage—Board Game by Brad Sugars
- *17 Ways to Increase Your Business Profits* booklet & tape by Brad Sugars. FREE OF CHARGE to Business Owners

*To order Brad Sugars' products from the recommended reading list, call your nearest *Action International* office today.

▌ The 18 Most Asked Questions about Working with an *Action International* Business Coach

And 18 great reasons why you'll jump at the chance to get your business flying and make your dreams come true

1. So who is *Action International?*

Action International is a business Coaching and Consulting company started in 1993 by entrepreneur and author Brad Sugars. With offices around the globe and business coaches from Singapore to Sydney to San Francisco, *Action International* has been set up with you, the business owner, in mind.

Unlike traditional consulting firms, *Action* is designed to give you both short-term assistance and long-term training through its affordable Mentoring approach. After 12 years teaching business owners how to succeed, *Action's* more than 10,000 clients and 1,000,000 seminar attendees will attest to the power of the programs.

Based on the sales, marketing, and business management systems created by Brad Sugars, your *Action* Coach is trained to not only show you how to increase your business revenues and profits, but also how to develop the business so that you as the owner work less and relax more.

Action International is a franchised company, so your local *Action* Coach is a fellow business owner who's invested her own time, money, and energy to make her business succeed. At *Action,* your success truly does determine our success.

2. And, why do I need a Business Coach?

Every great sports star, business person, and superstar is surrounded by coaches and advisors.

And, as the world of business moves faster and gets more competitive, it's difficult to keep up with both the changes in your industry and the innovations in sales, marketing, and management strategies. Having a business coach is no longer a luxury; it's become a necessity.

On top of all that, it's impossible to get an objective answer from yourself. Don't get me wrong. You can survive in business without the help of a Coach, but it's almost impossible to thrive.

A Coach *can* see the forest for the trees. A Coach will make you focus on the game. A Coach will make you run more laps than you feel like. A Coach will tell it like it is. A Coach will give you small pointers. A Coach will listen. A Coach will be your marketing manager, your sales director, your training coordinator, your partner, your confidant, your mentor, your best friend, and an *Action* Business Coach will help you make your dreams come true.

3. Then, what's an Alignment Consultation?

Great question. It's where an *Action* Coach starts with every business owner. You'll invest a minimum of $1295, and during the initial 2 to 3 hours your Coach invests with you, he'll learn as much as he can about your business, your goals, your challenges, your sales, your marketing, your finances, and so much more.

All with three goals in mind: To know exactly where your business is now. To clarify your goals both in the business and personally. And thirdly, to get the crucial pieces of information he needs to create your businesses *Action* Plan for the next 12 months.

Not a traditional business or marketing plan mind you, but a step-by-step plan of *Action* that you'll work through as you continue with the Mentor Program.

4. So, what, then, is the Mentor Program?

Simply put, it's where your *Action* Coach will work with you for a full 12 months to make your goals a reality. From weekly coaching calls and goal-setting sessions, to creating marketing pieces together, you will develop new sales strategies and business systems so you can work less and learn all that you need to know about how to make your dreams come true.

You'll invest between $995 and $10,000 a month and your Coach will dedicate a minimum of 5 hours a month to working with you on your sales, marketing, team building, business development, and every step of the *Action* Plan you created from your Alignment Consultation.

Unlike most consultants, your *Action* Coach will do more than just show you what to do. She'll be with you when you need her most, as each idea takes shape, as each campaign is put into place, as you need the little pointers on making it happen, when you need someone to talk to, when you're faced with challenges and, most importantly, when you're just not sure what to do next. Your Coach will be there every step of the way.

5. Why at least 12 months?

If you've been in business for more than a few weeks, you've seen at least one or two so called "quick fixes."

Most Consultants seem to think they can solve all your problems in a few hours or a few days. At *Action* we believe that long-term success means not just scraping the surface and doing it for you. It means doing it with you, showing you how to do it, working alongside you, and creating the success together.

Over the 12 months, you'll work on different areas of your business, and month by month you'll not only see your goals become a reality, you'll gain both the confidence and the knowledge to make it happen again and again, even when your first 12 months of Coaching is over.

6. How can you be sure this will work in my industry and in my business?

Very simple. You see at *Action*, we're experts in the areas of sales, marketing, business development, business management, and team building just to name a few. With 328 different profit-building strategies, you'll soon see just how powerful these systems are.

You, on the other hand, are the expert in your business and together we can apply the *Action* systems to make your business fly.

Add to this the fact that within the *Action* Team at least one of our Coaches has either worked with, managed, worked in, or even owned a business that's the same or very similar to yours. Your *Action* Coach has the full resources of the entire *Action* team to call upon for every challenge you have. Imagine hundreds of experts ready to help you.

7. Won't this just mean more work?

Of course when you set the plan with your *Action* Coach, it'll all seem like a massive amount of work, but no one ever said attaining your goals would be easy.

In the first few months, it'll take some work to adjust, some work to get over the hump so to speak. The further you are into the program, the less and less work you'll have to do.

You will, however, be literally amazed at how focused you'll be and how much you'll get done. With focus, an *Action* Coach, and most importantly the *Action* Systems, you'll be achieving a whole lot more with the same or even less work.

8. How will I find the time?

Once again the first few months will be the toughest, not because of an extra amount of work, but because of the different work. In fact, your *Action* Coach will show you how to, on a day-to-day basis, get more work done with less effort.

In other words, after the first few months you'll find that you're not working more, just working differently. Then, depending on your goals from about month six onwards, you'll start to see the results of all your work, and if you choose to, you can start working less than ever before. Just remember, it's about changing what you do with your time, *not* putting in more time.

9. How much will I need to invest?

Nothing, if you look at it from the same perspective as we do. That's the difference between a cost and an investment. Everything you do with your *Action* Coach is a true investment in your future.

Not only will you create great results in your business, but you'll end up with both an entrepreneurial education second to none, and the knowledge that you can repeat your successes over and over again.

As mentioned, you'll need to invest at least $1295 up to $5000 for the Alignment Consultation and Training Day, and then between $995 and $10,000 a month for the next 12 months of coaching.

Your Coach may also suggest several books, tapes, and videos to assist in your training, and yes, they'll add to your investment as you go. Why? Because having an *Action* Coach is just like having a marketing manager, a sales team leader, a trainer, a recruitment specialist, and corporate consultant all for half the price of a secretary.

10. Will it cost me extra to implement the strategies?

Once again, give your *Action* Coach just half an hour and he'll show you how to turn your marketing into an investment that yields sales and profits rather than just running up your expenses.

In most cases we'll actually save you money when we find the areas that aren't working for you. But yes, I'm sure you'll need to spend some money to make some money.

Yet, when you follow our simple testing and measuring systems, you'll never risk more than a few dollars on each campaign, and when we find the ones that work, we make sure you keep profiting from them time and again.

Remember, when you go the accounting way of saving costs, you can only ever add a few percent to the bottom line.

Following Brad Sugars' formula, your *Action* Coach will show you that through sales, marketing, and income growth, your possible returns are exponential.

The sky's the limit, as they say.

11. Are there any guarantees?

To put it bluntly, no. Your *Action* Coach will never promise any specific results, nor will she guarantee that any of your goals will become a reality.

You see, we're your coach. You're still the player, and it's up to you to take the field. Your Coach will push you, cajole you, help you, be there for you, and even do some things with you, but you've still got to do the work.

Only *you* can ever be truly accountable for your own success and at *Action* we know this to be a fact. We guarantee to give you the best service we can, to answer your questions promptly, and with the best available information. And, last but not least your *Action* Coach is committed to making you successful whether you like it or not.

That's right, once we've set the goals and made the plan, we'll do whatever it takes to make sure you reach for that goal and strive with all your might to achieve all that you desire.

Of course we'll be sure to keep you as balanced in your life as we can. We'll make sure you never compromise either the long-term health and success of your company or yourself, and more importantly your personal set of values and what's important to you.

12. What results have other business owners seen?

Anything from previously working 60 hours a week down to working just 10—right through to increases in revenues of 100s and even 1000s of percent. Results speak for themselves. Be sure to keep reading for specific examples of real people, with real businesses, getting real results.

There are three reasons why this will work for you in your business. Firstly, your *Action* Coach will help you get 100 percent focused on your goals and the step-by-step processes to get you there. This focus alone is amazing in its effect on you and your business results.

Secondly, your coach will hold you accountable to get things done, not just for the day-to-day running of the business, but for the dynamic growth of the business. You're investing in your success and we're going to get you there.

Thirdly, your Coach is going to teach you one-on-one as many of *Action's* 328 profit-building strategies as you need. So whether your goal is to be making more money, or working fewer hours or both inside the next 12 months your goals can become a reality. Just ask any of the thousands of existing *Action* clients, or more specifically, check out the results of 19 of our most recent clients shown later in this section.

13. What areas will you coach me in?

There are five main areas your *Action* Coach will work on with you. Of course, how much of each depends on you, your business, and your goals.

Sales. The backbone of creating a superprofitable business, and one area we'll help you get spectacular results in.

Marketing and Advertising. If you want to get a sale, you've got to get a prospect. Over the next 12 months your *Action* Coach will teach you Brad Sugars' amazingly simple streetwise marketing—marketing that makes profits.

Team Building and Recruitment. You'll never *wish* for the right people again. You'll have motivated and passionate team members when your Coach shows you how.

Systems and Business Development. Stop the business from running you and start running your business. Your Coach will show you the secrets to having the business work, even when you're not there.

Customer Service. How to deliver consistently, make it easy to buy, and leave your customers feeling delighted with your service. Both referrals and repeat business are centered in the strategies your Coach will teach you.

14. Can you also train my people?

Yes. We believe that training your people is almost as important as coaching you.

Your investment starts at $1500 for your entire team, and you can decide between five very powerful in-house training programs. From "*Sales Made Simple*" for your face-to-face sales team to "*Phone Power*" for your entire team's telephone etiquette and sales ability. Then you can run the *"Raving Fans"* customer service training or the *"Total Team"* training. And finally, if you're too busy earning a living to make any real money, then you've just got to attend our *"Business Academy 101."* It will make a huge impact on your finances, business, career, family, and lifestyle. You'll be amazed at how much involvement and excitement comes out of your team with each training program.

15. Can you write ads, letters, and marketing pieces for me?

Yes. Your *Action* Coach can do it for you, he can train you to do it yourself, or we can simply critique the marketing pieces you're using right now.

If you want us to do it for you, our one-time fees start at just $1195. You'll not only get one piece; we'll design several pieces for you to take to the market and see which one performs the best. Then, if it's a critique you're after, just $349 means we'll work through your entire piece and give you feedback on what to change, how to change it, and what else you should do. Last but not least, for between $15 and $795 we can recommend a variety of books, tapes, and most importantly, Brad Sugars' Instant Success series books that'll take you step-by-step through the how tos of creating your marketing pieces.

16. Why do you also recommend books, tapes, and videos?

Basically, to save you time and money. Take Brad Sugars' *Sales Rich* DVD or Video Series, for instance. In about 16 hours you'll learn more about business than you have in the last 12 years. It'll also mean your *Action* Coach works with you on the high-level implementation rather than the very basic teaching.

It's a very powerful way for you to speed up the coaching process and get phenomenal rather than just great results.

17. When is the best time to get started?

Yesterday. OK, seriously, right now, today, this minute, before you take another step, waste another dollar, lose another sale, work too many more hours, miss another family event, forget another special occasion.

Far too many business people wait and see. They think working harder will make it all better. Remember, what you know got you to where you are. To get to where you want to go, you've got to make some changes and most probably learn something new.

There's no time like the present to get started on your dreams and goals.

18. So how do we get started?

Well, you'd better get back in touch with your *Action* Coach. There's some very simple paperwork to sign, and then you're on your way.

You'll have to invest a few hours showing them everything about your business. Together you'll get a plan created and then the work starts. Remember, it may seem like a big job at the start, but with a Coach, you're sharing the load and together you'll achieve great things.

Here's what others say about what happened after working with an *Action* business coach

Paul and Rosemary Rose—Icontact Multimedia

"Our *Action* coach showed us several ways to help market our product. We went on to triple our client base and simultaneously tripled our profits in just seven months. It was unbelievable! Last year was our best Christmas ever. We were really able to spoil ourselves!"

S. Ford—Pride Kitchens

"In 6 months, I've gone from working more than 60 hours per week in my business to less than 20, and my conversion rate's up from 19 percent to 62 percent. I've now got some life back!"

Gary and Leanne Paper—Galea Timber Products

"We achieved our goal for the 12 months within a 6-month period with a 100 percent increase in turnover and a good increase in margins. We have already recommended and will continue to recommend this program to others."

Russell, Kevin, John, and Karen—Northern Lights Power and Distribution

"Our profit margin has increased from 8 percent to 21 percent in the last 8 months. *Action* coaching focussed us on what are our most profitable markets."

Ty Pedersen—De Vries Marketing Sydney

"After just three months of coaching, my sales team's conversion rate has grown from an average of less than 12 percent to more than 23 percent and our profits have climbed by more than 30 percent."

Hank Meerkerk and Hemi McGarvey—B.O.P. School of Welding

"Last year we started off with a profit forecast, but as soon as we got *Action* involved we decided to double our forecast. We're already well over that forecast again by two-and-a-half times on turnover, and profits are even higher. Now we run a really profitable business."

Stuart Birch—Education Personnel Limited

"One direct mail letter added $40,000 to my bottom line, and working with *Action* has given me quality time to work on my business and spend time with my family."

Mark West—Wests Pumping and Irrigation

"In four months two simple strategies have increased our business more than 20 percent. We're so busy, we've had to delay expanding the business while we catch up!"

Michael Griffiths—Gym Owner

"I went from working 70 hours per week *in* the business to just 25 hours, with the rest of the time spent working *on* the business."

Cheryl Standring—In Harmony Landscapes

"We tried our own direct mail and only got a 1 percent response. With *Action* our response rate increased to 20 percent. It's definitely worth every dollar we've invested."

Jason and Chris Houston—Empradoor Finishing

"After 11 months of working with *Action,* we have increased our sales by 497 percent, and the team is working without our having to be there."

Michael Avery—Coomera Pet Motels

"I was skeptical at first, but I knew we needed major changes in our business. In 2 months, our extra profits were easily covering our investment and our predictions for the next 10 months are amazing."

Garry Norris—North Tax & Accounting

"As an accountant, my training enables me to help other business people make more money. It is therefore refreshing when someone else can help me do the same. I have a policy of only referring my clients to people who are professional, good at what they do, and who have personally given me great service. *Action* fits all three of these criteria, and I recommend *Action* to my business clients who want to grow and develop their businesses further."

Lisa Davis and Steve Groves—Mt. Eden Motorcycles

"With *Action* we increased our database from 800 to 1200 in 3 months. We consistently get about 20 new qualified people on our database each week for less than $10 per week."

Christine Pryor—U-Name-It Embroidery

"Sales for August this year have increased 352 percent. We're now targeting a different market and we're a lot more confident about what we're doing."

Joseph Saitta and Michelle Fisher—Banyule Electrics

"Working with *Action,* our inquiry rate has doubled. In four months our business has changed so much our customers love us. It's a better place for people to work and our margins are widening."

Kevin and Alison Snook—Property Sales

"In the 12 months previous to working with *Action,* we had sold one home in our subdivision. In the first eight months of working with *Action,* we sold six homes. The results speak for themselves."

Wayne Manson—Hospital Supplies

"When I first looked at the Mentoring Program it looked expensive, but from the inside looking out, its been the best money I have ever spent. Sales are up more than $3000 per month since I started, and the things I have learned and expect to learn will ensure that I will enjoy strong sustainable growth in the future."

■ *Action* Contact Details

Action International Asia Pacific

Ground Floor, *Action* House, 2 Mayneview Street, Milton QLD 4064

Ph: +61 (0) 7 3368 2525

Fax: +61 (0) 7 3368 2535

Free Call: 1800 670 335

Action International Europe

Olympic House, Harbor Road, Howth, Co. Dublin, Ireland

Ph: +353 (0) 1-8320213

Fax: +353 (0) 1-8394934

Action International North America

5670 Wynn Road Suite A & C, Las Vegas, Nevada 89118

Ph: +1 (702) 795 3188

Fax: +1 (702) 795 3183

Free Call: (888) 483 2828

Action International UK

3-5 Richmond Hill, Richmond, Surrey, TW 106RE

Ph: +44 020 8948 5151

Fax: +44 020 8948 4111

Action Offices around the globe:

Australia | Canada | China | England | France | Germany | Hong Kong

India | Indonesia | Ireland | Malaysia | Mexico | New Zealand

Phillippines | Scotland | Spain | Singapore | USA | Wales

Here's how you can profit from all of Brad's ideas with your local *Action* International **Business Coach**

Just like a sporting coach pushes an athlete to achieve optimum performance, provides them with support when they are exhausted, and teaches the athlete to execute plays that the competition does not anticipate.

A business coach will make you run more laps than you feel like. A business coach will show it like it is. And a business coach will listen.

The role of an *Action* Business Coach is to show you how to improve your business through guidance, support, and encouragement. Your coach will help you with your sales, marketing, management, team building, and so much more. Just like a sporting coach, your *Action* Business Coach will help you and your business perform at levels you never thought possible.

Whether you've been in business for a week or 20 years, it's the right time to meet with and see how you'll profit from an *Action* Coach.

As the owner of a business it's hard enough to keep pace with all the changes and innovations going on in your industry, let alone to find the time to devote to sales, marketing, systems, planning and team management, and then to run your business as well.

As the world of business moves faster and becomes more competitive, having a Business Coach is no longer a luxury; it has become a necessity. Based on the sales, marketing, and business management systems created by Brad Sugars, your *Action* Coach is trained to not only show you how to increase your business revenues and profits but also how to develop your business so that you, as the owner, can take back control. All with the aim of your working less and relaxing more. Making money is one thing; having the time to enjoy it is another.

Your *Action* Business Coach will become your marketing manager, your sales director, your training coordinator, your confidant, your mentor. In short, your *Action* Coach will help you make your business dreams come true.

ATTENTION BUSINESS OWNERS
You can increase your profits now

Here's how you can have one of Brad's **Action** *International* Business Coaches guide you to success.

Like every successful sporting icon or team, a business needs a coach to help it achieve its full potential. In order to guarantee your business success, you can have one of Brad's team as your business coach. You will learn about how you can get amazing results with the help of the team at **Action** *International.*

The business coaches are ready to take you and your business on a journey that will reward you for the rest of your life. You see, we believe **Action** speaks louder than words.

Complete and post this card to your local **Action** office to discover how our team can help you increase your income today!

Action *International*

The World's Number-1 Business Coaching Team

Name ....

Position ....

Company ....

Address ....

....

Country ....

Phone ....

Fax ....

Email ....

Referred by ....

How do I become an *Action* *International* Business Coach?

If you choose to invest your time and money in a great business and you're looking for a white-collar franchise opportunity to build yourself a lifestyle, an income, a way to take control of your life and, a way to get great personal satisfaction …

Then you've just found the world's best team!

Now, it's about finding out if you've got what it takes to really enjoy and thrive in this amazing business opportunity.

Here are the 4 things we look for in every *Action* Coach:

1. You've got to love succeeding

We're looking for people who love success, who love getting out there and making things happen. People who enjoy mixing with other people, people who thrive on learning and growing, and people who want to charge an hourly rate most professionals only dream of.

2. You've got to love being in charge of your own life

When you're ready to take control, the key is to be in business for yourself, but not by yourself. *Action*'s support, our training, our world leading systems, and the backup of a global team are all waiting to give you the best chance of being an amazing business success.

3. You've got to love helping people

Being a great Coach is all about helping yourself by helping others. The first time clients thank you for showing them step by step how to make more money and work less within their business, will be the day you realize just how great being an *Action* Business Coach really is.

4. You've got to love a great lifestyle

Working from home, setting your own timetable, spending time with family and friends, knowing that the hard work you do is for your own company and, not having to climb a so-called corporate ladder. This is what lifestyle is all about. Remember, business is supposed to give you a life, not take it away.

Our business is booming and we're seriously looking for people ready to find out more about how becoming a member of the *Action* *International* Business Coaching team is going to be the best decision you've ever made.

Apply online now at www.action-international.com

Here's how you can network, get new leads, build yourself an instant sales team, learn, grow and build a great team of supportive business owners around you by checking into your local *Action* Profit Club

Joining your local *Action* Profit Club is about more than just networking, it's also the learning and exchanging of profitable ideas.

Embark on a journey to a more profitable enterprise by meeting with fellow, like-minded business owners.

An *Action* Profit Club is an excellent way to network with business people and business owners. You will meet every two weeks for breakfast to network and learn profitable strategies to grow your business.

Here are three reasons why *Action International's* Profit Clubs work where other networking groups don't:

1. You know networking is a great idea. The challenge is finding the time and maintaining the motivation to keep it up and make it a part of your business. If you're not really having fun and getting the benefits, you'll find it gets easier to find excuses that stop you going. So, we guarantee you will always have fun and learn a lot from your bi-weekly group meetings.
2. The real problem is that so few people do any work 'on' their business. Instead they generally work "in" it, until it's too late. By being a member of an *Action* Profit Club, you get to attend FREE business-building workshops run by Business Coaches that teach you how to work "on" your business and avoid this common pitfall and help you to grow your business.
3. Unlike other groups, we have marketing systems to assist in your groups' growth rather than just relying on you to bring in new members. This way you can concentrate on YOUR business rather than on ours.

Latest statistics show that the average person knows at least 200 other contacts. By being a member of your local *Action* Profit Club, you have an instant network of around 3,000 people

Join your local *Action* Profit Club today.

Apply online now at www.actionprofitclub.com

LEVERAGE—The Game of Business
Your Business Success is just a Few Games Away

Leverage—The Game of Business is a fun way to learn how to succeed in business fast.

The rewards start flowing the moment you start playing!

Leverage is three hours of fun, learning, and discovering how you can be an amazingly successful business person.

It's a breakthrough in education that will have you racking up the profits in no time. The principles you take away from playing this game will set you up for a life of business success. It will open your mind to what's truly possible. Apply what you learn and **sit back and watch your profits soar.**

By playing this fun and interactive business game, you will learn:

- How to quickly raise your business income
- How business people can become rich and successful in a short space of time
- How to create a business that works without you

Isn't it time you had the edge over your competition?

Leverage has been played by all age groups from 12-85 and has been a huge learning experience for all. The most common comment we hear is: 'I thought I knew a lot, and just by playing a simple board game I have realized I have a long way to go. The knowledge I've gained from playing Leverage will make me thousands! Thanks for the lesson.'

To order your copy online today, please visit www.bradsugars.com

Also available in the

THE BUSINESS COACH
Learn how to master the six steps on
the ladder of success

(0-07-146672-X)

INSTANT REPEAT BUSINESS
Build a solid and loyal
customer base

(0-07-146666-5)

THE REAL ESTATE COACH
Invest in real estate with
little or no cash

(0-07-146662-2)

INSTANT SALES
Master the crucial first minute of
any sales call

(0-07-146664-9)

INSTANT PROMOTIONS
Create powerful press releases, amazing
ads, and brilliant brochures

(0-07-146665-7)

INSTANT
SUCCESS
Real Results. Right Now.

Instant Success series.

INSTANT CASHFLOW
Turn every lead into a sale

(0-07-146659-2)

BILLIONAIRE IN TRAINING
Learn the wealth building secrets
of billionaires

(0-07-146661-4)

INSTANT PROFIT
Boost your bottom line with
a cash-building plan

(0-07-146668-1)

SUCCESSFUL FRANCHISING
Learn how to buy or sell a franchise

(0-07-146671-1)

INSTANT ADVERTISING
Create ads that stand out and sell

(0-07-146660-6)

INSTANT REFERRALS
Never cold call or chase after
customers again

(0-07-146667-3)

INSTANT LEADS
Generate a steady flow of leads

(0-07-146663-0)

INSTANT SYSTEMS
Stop running your business and start
growing it

(0-07-146670-3)

INSTANT TEAM BUILDING
Learn the six keys to a winning team

(0-07-146669-X)

*Your source for the strategies, skills,
and confidence every business owner
needs to succeed.*